What'll We Talk About?

A VOCABULARY AND CONVERSATION BOOK

Jeanne Handschuh

Alma Simounet-Géigel

UNIVERSITY OF PUERTO RICO

Illustrations by Brenda Meléndez and Ananelis Ramos

REGENTS / PRENTICE HALL Englewood Cliffs, New Jersey 07632

Library of Congress Cataloging-in-Publication Data

Handschuh, Jeanne, date.
    What'll we talk about? : a vocabulary and conversation book /
Jeanne Handschuh, Alma Simounet-Géigel ; illustrations by Brenda
Meléndez and Ananelis Ramos.
    ISBN 0-13-951096-6
    1. English language—Textbooks for foreign speakers. 2. English
language—Conversation and phrase books. 3. Vocabulary.
I. Simounet-Géigel, Alma, date. II. Title.
PE1128.H264   1992
428.3'4—dc20
                                            92-3268
                                            CIP

Acquisitions editor: *Anne Riddick*
Editorial/production supervision, interior design, and photo research: *Louise B. Capuano*
Desktop production supervision: *Molly Pike Riccardi, Shari Toron*
Cover design: *Bruce Kenselaar*
Chapter opening layouts: *Anne Ricigliano (designer), Meg Van Arsdale, Pete Ticola, Karen Noferi*
Computer art (Chap. 3): *Warren Fischbach*
Pre-press buyer: *Ray Keating*
Manufacturing buyer: *Lori Bulwin*
Scheduler: *Leslie Coward*

© 1992 by REGENTS/PRENTICE HALL
A Division of Simon & Schuster
Englewood Cliffs, New Jersey 07632

Photo Credits appear on page 232.

Printed in the United States of America

10   9   8   7   6   5   4

ISBN 0-13-951096-6

Prentice-Hall International (UK) Limited, *London*
Prentice-Hall of Australia Pty. Limited, *Sydney*
Prentice-Hall Canada Inc., *Toronto*
Prentice-Hall Hispanoamericana, S.A., *Mexico*
Prentice-Hall of India Private Limited, *New Delhi*
Prentice-Hall of Japan, Inc., *Tokyo*
Simon & Schuster Asia Pte. Ltd., *Singapore*
Editora Prentice-Hall do Brasil, Ltda., *Rio de Janeiro*

We dedicate this book to our husbands,
Robert Handschuh and Wilfredo Géigel,
for their patience and support; to Eugenio;
and to our students at UPR, from whom
we are constantly learning.

CONTENTS

PREFACE

Intermediate and advanced students of English as a second language often complain that although they have spent several years studying the language, their command of English vocabulary is limited. At professional meetings, ESL teachers frequently bring up the same problem. The use of the communicative approach to teaching language has spotlighted this situation by introducing students to a variety of activities that require the knowledge of a specific vocabulary. Students who lack this important tool for interaction feel uncomfortable and often become frustrated because, although they welcome an opportunity to communicate in English, they realize that they are ill-equipped to do so.

With this problem in mind, and based on the experience we have gained from more than twenty-five years of teaching ESL students, we decided to write a textbook implementing the communicative approach, which would enable students to increase their English vocabulary within the context of specific thematic areas relative to their own lives. Then, equipped with a knowledge of appropriate vocabulary, ESL students who found themselves in a situation where communication in English was a necessity could experience success instead of failure. A glance at the Table of Contents will reveal that great care has been taken to concentrate on specific themes or topics of interest to students.

In selecting the vocabulary items to be covered in each lesson, we felt the list should not be limited to words alone, but should also include two-word verbs and certain idiomatic expressions which are an integral part of the English language. These expressions can be very confusing to ESL students, especially when the items are presented out of context, as so often happens in ESL texts, or when students are not given the opportunity to practice using them in communicative situations. In *What'll We Talk About?*, the usage of the vocabulary items is based on information contained in the following: *Webster's New World Dictionary,* Second College Edition (New York: Simon & Schuster, 1984) and *The Longman Dictionary of Phrasal Verbs,* edited by Rosemary Courtney (Essex, England: Longman Group, 1983).

What'll We Talk About? consists of 14 lessons, two of which are review, and an appendix which explains the uses of cardinal and ordinal numbers. (Scripts for the Listening Comprehension Exercises are also included.) The lessons comprise the following sections:

1. DIALOGUES using carefully selected vocabulary items in realistic natural-sounding speech. Students should, in most cases, be able to figure out the meaning of the words and idiomatic expressions from the way in which these items are used in the dialogues. (Cassettes of the dialogues, recorded by native speakers, are available.)

2. QUESTIONS ABOUT THE DIALOGUES not only cover content, but also stimulate critical thinking and class discussion.

3. QUESTIONS FOR CLASS DISCUSSION based on students' own experiences give them an opportunity to express their opinions on the topic being discussed.

4. HOMEWORK EXERCISES which require students to use selected vocabulary items in semi-constructed dialogues, substitution exercises, and in original sentences or dialogues. The purpose of these exercises is, of course, to reinforce the information covered in the lesson.

5. LISTENING COMPREHENSION EXERCISES in which students listen to dialogues or sentences using selected vocabulary studied in the lesson and answer multiple-choice questions.

6. CONVERSATION PRACTICE which offers students the chance to use vocabulary learned in the lesson in role-playing activities based on real-life situations relative to their own needs and experience.

What'll We Talk About? is intended for intermediate or advanced students of English as a second language. The lessons do not have to be taught in consecutive order, and, although the book is designed for a full semester, it can be used effectively in a shorter course by selecting those lessons considered most important to a particular culture or teaching situation. In fact, the book can be used in any course which attempts to provide ESL students with experience in communication, with a special emphasis on the expansion of the learner's knowledge of English vocabulary in context. The text is designed to be used anywhere in the world — wherever English is taught as either a foreign, a second, or an auxiliary language. A detailed Instructor's Manual is available. It provides ideas for teaching procedures, as well as a lesson-by-lesson discussion of additional suggestions related to various types of practice, such as reading and writing activities, other topics for class discussion, supplementary lists of vocabulary, grammar pointers, and culture capsules.

There are several people to whom we owe our gratitude for their help in making our book a reality. Therefore, we would like to extend our sincere thanks and appreciation to the following: our former colleague at UPR, Eleanor Lawton Sebeok, for her detailed comments on the earliest version of the manuscript; Norma Maurosa, for typing all the various drafts; Ivan Bustamante, Regents/Prentice Hall sales representative in San Juan, for his wise counsel on various occasions; and, finally, our editors at Regents/Prentice Hall, especially Louise B. Capuano, our production editor. We wish to express our special gratitude to Tina Carver for suggesting that we write a vocabulary/conversation book, and for her continuing encouragement, interest, and support.

Jeanne Handschuh

Alma Simounet-Géigel

1

Getting to Know You

1

EXPLANATION OF TWO-WORD VERBS

Throughout this textbook you will learn many combinations of verbs plus prepositions or adverbs. These verbs are usually referred to as *two-word verbs,* though some of the verbs have *three* words. (**Run out of** is an example of a three-word verb.) Some of these verbs are "inseparable." That means that *the first word may not be separated from the second.* (**Run into** is an example of an *inseparable verb.*) Other two-word verbs, however, are "separable." This means that the first element may be separated from the second by either a noun or a pronoun. (**Pick up** is an example of a *separable verb.*)

> **NOTE:** While the noun may also follow the second element, a pronoun always comes between the two parts of a separable verb. However, if the verb is inseparable or has three elements, both the noun and the pronoun follow the complete verb.

Study these dialogues between Student **A** and Student **B** and you will understand how the separable and inseparable verbs are used.

1. **A:** I'm going to the library. Want to come with me?

   B: Sorry. I can't. I'm in a hurry to get home. If you **run into** my friend Abdul, please give him my regards. He works at the circulation desk.

   A: As a matter of fact, I **ran into** him just yesterday. He wants you to call him.

Since **run into** is an inseparable verb, both the noun **friend** and the pronoun **him** follow the complete verb.

2. **A:** Have you bought the history book yet?

   B: I'm on my way to the bookstore to **pick up** the book right now. Do you need anything?

   A: Could you **pick up** some typing paper for me? I'm **running out of** it.

   B: Sure. I'll be glad to **pick** some **up** for you.

As you can see, **pick up** is a separable verb and **run out of** is an inseparable verb. In this particular dialogue, the nouns **book** and **typing paper** follow the complete verb, while the pronoun **some** comes between the word **pick** and **up**. However, since **run out of** is inseparable, the pronoun **it** follows the complete verb.

Dialogue 3 gives you another example of separable two-word verbs.

3. **A:** Did you **take** the dishes **out** of the dishwasher?

   B: Yes, I **took** them **out** and **put** them **back** in the cabinet.

In this dialogue, both the noun and the pronoun separate the two parts of the verb.

4. A: I'm going to stay at home this weekend. I don't want to **get behind in** my assignments.

B: I know what you mean. I don't like to **get behind in** them either. It's too hard to **catch up with** the class.

Did you notice that **get behind in** and **catch up with** are inseparable? Also, did you notice that, since they have *three* words, both the noun and the pronoun follow the complete verb?

When pronouncing the two-word verbs, put the primary (strong) stress on the second element because that's the part which gives the verb its particular meaning.

Examples: run ínto, run óut of.

> **NOTE:** Throughout the textbook, separable verbs will be followed by (S):
>
> **pick up** (S) **take (took) out** (S)
>
> If a two-word verb is irregular, we have included its past tense form in the vocabulary list for the dialogue in which the verb first appears. If you don't already know this form, learn it along with the meaning of the verb.
>
> **take (took) out** (S)
>
> When a verb is written with a dash between the elements this indicates the two elements are *usually* separated by a noun or pronoun.
>
> *Examples:* **do — good** (S) **put — to bed** (S)

DIALOGUES

The boldface words and expressions used in these dialogues should become part of your English vocabulary. You will probably be able to learn their meanings from the way in which they are used in the various dialogues.

1. A: I **had a good time** at the welcome-back party. There were a lot of people there. I met **quite a few** people I didn't know before.

B: I did too. And I **ran into** a friend I hadn't seen since **grade school.** We **made a date** for lunch next Saturday. Want to come with us?

A: Next Saturday? Sorry, I can't **make it.** I have a one o'clock class. Thanks anyway.

B: That's too bad. Maybe next time. Well, I have to go now. Bye, bye.

Questions

1. What do you think **A** means by "quite a few people"?
2. What's another way of saying "I ran into a friend"?
3. How else can you say "we made a date"?
4. What does **A** mean by "sorry, I can't make it"?
5. Who do you think the speakers are? How can you tell?

2. Francisco: Professor, excuse me. What does "given name" mean?

   B: It's your first name. Francisco is your **given name**.

Francisco: OK. I understand. I know my **last name** is my **family name,** but what is my **surname**?

   B: It's your family name, too. Surname, family name, last name — they all mean the same thing. Your surname is García. Your first name together with your family name is your **full name.** Can you tell me your full name?

Francisco: U-um-m. Francisco José García. José's my **middle name.** What's a **nickname**?

   B: It's a name your family or your friends call you instead of your first name. If a man is named Richard, his friends might call him Dick or Richie. Do you have a nickname, Francisco?

Francisco: Well, my American friends call me Frank. I'm **named after** my father. Everybody calls him Don Paco, so they call me Paquito.

Questions

1. What is the student's full name?
2. What does Francisco mean when he says he's named after his father?
3. What are his nicknames? What is his middle name?
4. What is Francisco's ethnic background? How do you know?

Making an Informal Introduction

3. A: Hi, Dick. How're you doing?

   B: Not bad, but I'm sure **looking forward to** that holiday next Monday. I can use a **long weekend** to **catch up with** my assignments. I was sick last week and I **got behind in** my lab work. How about you? How're things going this semester?

   A: OK, so far. Dick, this is my **roommate,** Jill Evans. Jill, this is a friend of mine, Dick Mason. We're from the same **hometown.** We went all through school together.

   B: Hi, Jill. Glad to meet you.

   C: Nice to meet you, too. You mentioned lab work. Are you a biology **major**?

B: No, I'm a pre-med major. Well, excuse me. I have to get over to the lab and **get started**. Nice meeting you, Jill. Hope I'll see you around.

A: So long. Take care.

C: Bye, Dick.

Questions

1. What does the expression **look forward to** mean in this dialogue?
2. Why does Dick refer to next weekend as a "long weekend"?
3. What does **B** mean by "we went all through school together"?
4. Is **B** male or female? What makes you think so?
5. During which part of the semester does this conversation take place? Why do you think so?
6. What's another way of saying **get started**?

Introducing Yourself and Starting a Conversation

4. **A:** Hi, there. Aren't you in my English class?

B: English 231, Section 5? I thought you **looked familiar**. My name's Michelle Wilkins.

A: I'm Luis Rodríguez. I'm on my way to the **snack bar** for a cup of coffee. Care to join me?

B: Thanks, Luis. I'd love to but I can't. I'm **in a hurry** to get to the bookstore before it closes. I have to **pick up** a book for my psychology class. Can I **take a rain check** for some other time? Maybe tomorrow — after class?

A: OK. Sure. Anytime. It's Michelle Williams. Right?

B: Wilkins. My friends call me Micki.

A: Micki Wilkins. OK. I've **got** your name **straight** now. So long. See you in class tomorrow.

B: Right. Bye, Luis.

Questions

1. What does Michelle mean when she says that Luis looks familiar?
2. How else could Michelle have said "I have to pick up a book"?
3. What does Luis mean when he asks "care to join me?"
4. What does Michelle mean when she asks "can I take a rain check?" Why do you think she said that to Luis?
5. What does Luis mean when he says "I've got your name straight now"?

5. **A:** Excuse me. Do you know which building is the **College** of Engineering?

B: I'm sorry. I don't know. I'm new here. This is my first day on **campus**.

A: I'm new here too. Where are you from?

B: Well, I was born in Shanghai, but when I was two years old we — my family — moved to Hong Kong. That was twenty years ago. So I guess I'm from Hong Kong. Where are you from?

A: Berlin. **By the way**, my name's Werner Straus.

B: I'm Kim Chang. Glad to meet you. What are you **majoring in**?

A: Civil engineering. And you?

B: Psychology. I'm in the College of Social Science. I'm a transfer student from the state **university**.

A: Excuse me. I think that's the **Dean** of Students Office over there. Maybe I can **find out** where the College of Engineering is.

B: Your name again?

A: Werner Straus. And yours?

B: Kim Chang.

A: Glad to meet you, Kim. Hope we'll meet again.

B: Same here. So long.

Questions

1. In what country was Kim Chang born? What is his nationality?
2. Do you know where Hong Kong is? What do you know about its history?
3. How old is Kim? How do you know?
4. What country is Werner from?
5. What word could you substitute for **college** in this dialogue?
6. What's the difference between a college and a university?
7. What is a transfer student?

A More Formal Introduction

6. **A:** Hello, Jane. How are you?

B: Oh, hello, Sarah. How're you **getting along**?

A: Pretty well, thanks. I'm gradually **learning my way around** the campus.

B: Sarah, I'd like you to meet my husband, Dr. Frank Wilson. Frank, this is my **colleague**, Professor Sarah Whitmore. Sarah's my new **officemate**.

A: **How do you do**, Dr. Wilson? It's a pleasure to meet you.

C: The pleasure is mine. You know, my mother's **maiden name** was Whitmore. You're not by any chance from California, are you?

A: No, sir. I'm not. My family's from London.

C: That's a long way from California, isn't it? Well, Sarah, I'm very glad to have met you. I hope we'll meet again soon. Good night.

A: Thank you, Dr. Wilson. I hope so too. Good night.

B: See you on Wednesday, Sarah.

NOTE TO THE STUDENT:

1. The expression **How do you do?** is used *only* when meeting someone for the first time in a formal situation.

2. When you are introduced to someone, you do not usually say "How are you?" or "How are you doing?" These and similar expressions are used when greeting someone you already know. Young people, however, do sometimes use these expressions in an informal situation.

3. When you are introduced to someone, it's a good idea to repeat that person's name, especially if it is an unusual name or one that is difficult for you to pronounce. You can also ask the person to spell his or her name as you write it down. This may help you remember the name better.

Questions

1. What is another way of asking "How are you getting along?"
2. How do you know that this is Sarah's first semester on campus?
3. How do you know that both women probably teach in the same department?
4. What country is Professor Whitmore's family from? What is their nationality? *(There are two ways of expressing it.)*
5. Do you think that Dr. Wilson is an older person? Why do you think so?

VOCABULARY

All of the words and idiomatic expressions listed on page 8 have been used in the dialogues of this lesson. You will be using some of them to answer the Questions for Class Discussion. Both the homework assignment and the listening comprehension exercise require knowledge of some of these vocabulary items. You have probably been able to learn the meanings of most of the words and expressions from observing the way in which they are used in the various dialogues. The vocabulary items are listed according to the dialogue in which they appear. Study them carefully. They should all become part of your English vocabulary.

DIALOGUE 1

grade (*or* elementary *or* grammar) school
quite a few
have a good time
make it
make (made) a date
run (ran) into – meet by chance,
    accidentally

DIALOGUE 2

given name (names)
last name, family name
surname
full name
middle name
nickname
be named after (S) – have the same
    name as (S)

DIALOGUE 3

roommate
hometown
long weekend
major – field of study, concentration
catch (caught) up with
get (got) behind in
get (got) started
look forward to

DIALOGUE 4

snack bar
in a hurry
take (took) a rain check
get (got) (something) straight (S)
pick up (S)
look familiar

DIALOGUE 5

dean
college (*also* school *or* faculty)
university
campus
by the way
major in (v)
find (found) out (S)

DIALOGUE 6

colleague
officemate
maiden name
get (got) along
learn (my, your, his, her, etc.) way
    around (S)
How do you do?

QUESTIONS FOR CLASS DISCUSSION

Assuming that you and your classmates are seated in a semicircle, ask the person sitting next to you *the first four questions* in the following manner. Be sure to speak in a voice loud enough for all your classmates to hear, and remember to look at the person to whom you are speaking. Use short answers. For example, in answer to a question like "Where are you from?" you'd say "Chicago," or "Bangkok," or whatever city you come from.

> *Example:* **Student A:** What's your full name?
> **Student B:** Jaime Garcia.
> **Student A:** Where are you from?
> **Student B:** Taiwan.

Student A: What college are you studying in?
Student B: Natural Sciences.
Student A: What are you majoring in?
Student B: Chemistry.

Student **B** will ask the student next to him the same questions and so on around the class. After everyone has asked and answered the first four questions, see how many students' names you can remember.

1. What's your full name?

2. Where are you from? *(city, town, or country, depending upon where the class is being given)*

3. What college or school are you studying in? *(Natural Science, Humanities, Music, etc.)*

4. What are you majoring in? *(That is, what do you plan to specialize in?)*

NOTE TO INSTRUCTOR: You may or may not want to have each student ask the remaining questions in round-robin fashion, depending on the amount of class time you have. Also, if you plan to teach the lesson in cardinal and ordinal numbers (Appendix), you may want to save Question 6 to use with that lesson.

---

5. How long have you been studying English?

6. What is your local address and telephone number? *(See the Appendix for the correct way to give your address if you are not sure.)*

7. Does your mother use her maiden name or her married name?

8. Are you named after anyone? If so, explain.

9. Does either your first name or your last name mean anything? *(For example, the first name Lily [a name of a flower] or the last name Shoemaker [one who makes shoes].)*

10. Does anyone in your family have what you consider to be an unusual name? Explain why you think so.

11. Do you have a nickname? If so, can you explain the origin of your nickname?

HOMEWORK

A. Incomplete Dialogues

Complete these dialogues using expressions you have learned in this lesson. Refer to the dialogues in this lesson for suggestions. In some you will have to supply appropriate answers. In others you will supply the questions. When you are finished writing the dialogues, practice reading them aloud. If you have the opportunity, read them with another student.

Informal Greeting: Saying Hello and Goodbye

1. **A:** Hi, _____ . How's it going?
               (name)

       B: Pretty _____ . And how about you?

       A: _____ , thanks. Well, _____ , I have to go now.
                                                  (B's name)

           It was good _____ you. _____ later.

       B: Same here. So _____ . Take _____ .

2. **A:** Hi , _____ . How're _____ ?

       B: Not bad, thank you. How _____ ?

       A: Pretty well. Sorry, I have _____ now. I'm in a hurry.

           It was nice _____ you. So long.

       B: Nice seeing you, too. _____ .

Greeting a Friend and Saying Goodbye

3. **A:** Hi, _____ . Did you have a good time at the
               (name)

           _____ party?

       B: Yes, _____ . How about you?

       A: I _____ , too. Well, I have _____ now.

       B: Me, too. I'll _____ later.

Informal Introduction

4. **A:** Hello, _____ . How are you? This is my friend
               (name)

           _____ .
           (name)

       B: Hi, _____ , I'm glad _____ you.
              (name of friend)

       C: Hi, _____ , I'm glad _____ you, too.
             (B's name)

Formal Introduction

5. **A:** _____ , I'd like you _____ Professor Jackson.
(name)

Professor Jackson, this is my friend, _____ .

B: How _____ , Professor Jackson? It's _____

to meet you.

C: *(Professor Jackson)* It's a pleasure _____ , too,

_____ .
(B's name)

B. Vocabulary Building

Reread the dialogues carefully. Then use these words and expressions in original sentences or dialogues. Be sure that in the sentences or dialogues you write the meanings of the expressions you use will be understood by the reader. *When an expression has more than one meaning, use the meaning discussed in this lesson.* Underline the expressions.

take a rain check
quite a few
look forward to – anticipate happily
(to be) in a hurry
make a date
look familiar
get —— straight – to understand
    something . . . finally)
learn (my, your, his, etc.) way around

college, university *(choose one)*
get behind in
catch up with
find out (S)
run into – to meet by chance,
    unexpectedly
pick up (S) – to obtain, buy
major in

LISTENING COMPREHENSION EXERCISE: STUDENT'S ANSWER SHEET

After listening to the questions concerning the dialogues, put a check (✔) on the line next to the sentence in each group that you think is the best answer.

Practice Dialogue

_____ **a)** I'd like you to prepare the lunch.

_____ **b)** I'd like you to bring a present.

_____ **c)** I'd like you to come.

1. _____ **a)** It is an informal way of saying hello.

_____ **b)** They are being introduced to one another.

_____ **c)** One person is asking the other how she feels.

2. _____ **a)** collect.

_____ **b)** look for.

_____ **c)** buy.

3. _____ **a)** a rather large number.

_____ **b)** not very many.

_____ **c)** almost none.

4. _____ **a)** I can't. I have to cash a check.

_____ **b)** I'll go if it doesn't rain.

_____ **c)** I can't go now, but I'd like to go some other time.

5. _____ **a)** I'll be able to go home.

_____ **b)** I want very much to go home.

_____ **c)** I have to go home.

6. _____ **a)** We'll look at the calendar.

_____ **b)** We'll arrange to meet.

_____ **c)** We'll prepare lunch.

7. _____ **a)** I hit them with the bike.

_____ **b)** I met them by chance.

_____ **c)** I arranged to meet them.

8. _____ **a)** a field or open space outside of a city.

_____ **b)** the grounds of a university or college.

_____ **c)** a place to go camping.

9. _____ **a)** a word referring to an unmarried woman.

_____ **b)** a woman's name before she is married.

_____ **c)** a nickname.

10. _____ **a)** We're both members of the same sports organization.

_____ **b)** We're both students at the university.

_____ **c)** We both teach at the university.

CONVERSATION PRACTICE

1. Using one of the following expressions, start a conversation with someone in the class you do not know. Have a short conversation during which you introduce yourself. End the conversation by using an appropriate expression to say goodbye. Practice the conversation so that you can present it to the class if the instructor asks you and your friend to do so.

In a classroom

Excuse me, is this English _____ , Section _____ ?

In a cafeteria

Pardon me. Is this seat taken?

At a bus stop

Have you been waiting long?

On a street corner

Excuse me, is this where I can get a train (bus) to _____ ?

Standing in line at a bank or bookstore

Aren't you in my _____ class?

Walking on the campus

Hello. I think we live in the same building (apartment building; boarding house).

Standing in line at a cafeteria

Pardon me, but you look very familiar. Haven't we met before?

Outside a classroom

Excuse me, do you have a match (for a cigarette)?

In a classroom, waiting room, bus station, etc.

It's very hot (cold) in here, isn't it?

2. Following your instructor's directions, form a group with two other students and practice introducing one of the people listed in Column A to the person listed opposite in Column B. Use some of the expressions you have learned in the preceding dialogues. Some of the combinations of A and B require formal expressions; others call for more informal expressions. End the conversation in an appropriate manner. Practice the dialogue several times so that you can present it to the class.

COLUMN A	COLUMN B
your instructor	your mother who is a judge
one friend	another friend
your kid brother or sister	your classmate
your boyfriend or girlfriend	your parents
your mother or father (or both)	the dean of your college
your friend	your English instructor
a friend	your grandfather, Dr. _____

3. When your instructor asks everyone to stand up and walk around, find someone you do not know and introduce yourself. Sit down with that person and find out as much as you can about him or her in five minutes. Take notes so that you can report your findings to the class. Be sure to mention the person's full name when you make your report. Limit your report to two or three minutes.

NOTE TO THE INSTRUCTOR: This activity could be more time-consuming than the other two. It also requires more language competency.

2

Getting Acquainted with Classroom Jargon

DIALOGUES

As you study these dialogues, pay particular attention to the boldface words and phrases. They are the vocabulary items for this lesson. You should be able to tell what they mean from the way in which they are used in the dialogues.

1. **Instructor:** Good morning. Robert, will you please **erase** the board for me?

Robert: Of course.

Instructor: Hana, will you please **pass out** these **index cards**?

Hana: I'll be glad to.

Instructor: When you get the card, please **print** your name — last name first — in the **upper left-hand corner**. In the **upper right-hand** corner, write your student number. (Demonstrates with card.) Please write **in ink**. Yes, Ning?

Ning: (Raising her hand.) Excuse me, what does **print** mean?

Instructor: Oh. It means to write your name like this. (Demonstrates on board.) Understand? Then **skip a line** and write your **permanent address**. Skip another line and write your **local address** and telephone number. Yes, Frederick?

Frederick: I'm sorry. I don't understand. What do you mean when you say "skip a line"?

Instructor: I want you to **write on every other line**. Like this. (Demonstrates on board.)

Frederick: Thank you.

Instructor: When you finish, **pass** your card **to the right**. I'll collect the cards from the person at the end of the **row**.

Questions

1. What did the professor ask Robert to do?
2. What information did the students have to write on the index cards?
3. Why do you think the instructor asked the students to write both their permanent and local (temporary) addresses?
4. What's another way of saying "skip a line"?
5. What is the meaning of **row** in this dialogue?

NOTE TO THE STUDENT: A teacher should never be addressed as "teacher." A high-school or grade-school teacher is addressed as Mr., Mrs., Miss, or Ms., plus the surname. A person who teaches in a college or a university is referred to as an instructor or professor. This person may be addressed as Dr., Miss, Ms., Mrs., or Mr., plus the surname, according to his or her personal preference. "Professor" may be used with or without the surname.

2. **Instructor:** Is there anyone who's here for the first time today? No one? OK. I'm going to **call the roll** from the cards you **filled out** last time. I haven't had time to put your names in my **rollbook** yet. (Addressing a student.) Yes? Do you have a question?

Student: I was here last time, but I **came in** late. I didn't **fill out** the card.

Instructor: OK. Come and get a card. I'll explain how to fill it out.

Student: (Picking up card.) Thank you.

Instructor: Maria, does your last name begin with a **G** or **J**?

Maria: **J**.

Instructor: And what's your **student number**? I can't **make out** your **handwriting**.

Maria: 806 89 3215

Instructor: 806 89 3215. Thank you, Maria.

Questions

1. What is another way of saying "call the roll"?
2. Where is the professor going to write the students' names?
3. What does one student tell the professor?
4. What's the professor's response?
5. Why do you think the student arrived late?
6. With which letter does Maria's last name begin?
7. Which letter comes first in the English alphabet—**J** or **G**?
8. Why does the professor ask Maria for her student number?
9. What is Maria's student number?
10. Do you know another word for **handwriting**?

3. **Instructor:** Luis, where is your **textbook**? Did you lose it?

Luis: I'm sorry, professor. I forgot to bring it this morning. I left it on my desk at home.

Instructor: Well, **look on with** Eric today. Please remember to bring your book next time.

Luis: I will.

Instructor: There's a **mistake** in Exercise 3 on page 5. In sentence number 2, **cross out** the word *and*.

Thomas: Excuse me. What do you mean by **cross out**?

Instructor: To cross out a word or sentence means to put an **X** through the word or to **draw a line through** it. Like this. (Demonstrates on board.)

Thomas: Thank you. I thought that's what it meant, but I wanted to **make sure**.

Questions

1. Why doesn't Luis have his textbook this morning?
2. What does the instructor tell Luis to do so that he can follow the lesson?
3. What does the instructor tell Luis to remember?
4. Why do you think Luis forgot to bring his textbook?
5. What does **look on with** mean?
6. Why does the instructor ask the students to cross out the word **and**?
7. What's another word for **mistake**?
8. What's another way of saying **cross out**?
9. What did Thomas mean when he said he wanted to "make sure"?

4. **Instructor:** **Take out** your textbook and open it to page 10. I'm going to read the sentences. In each sentence there are two words in **parentheses**. When I read the sentence, I'll read only one of the words. **Circle** the word that you hear. Understand? If you don't, please **raise your hand**. Yes, Pierre?

    Pierre: I'm sorry. I don't know what you mean by "circle the word."

Instructor: I mean, **draw a line**, a circle, **around** the word. Like this. (Demonstrates on board.) Are there any other questions? OK. Let's begin. I'll read each sentence twice.

Questions

1. What are the first instructions that the professor gives the students?
2. What's the instructor going to do?
3. What does the instructor tell the students to do if they don't understand the instructions?
4. What's another way of saying "draw a circle around"?
5. Why do you think the instructor is going to read each sentence two times?

5. **Instructor:** I'm going to write the **homework assignment** on the **chalkboard**. Please **copy** it in your **notebook**. Yes?

    Student: (Raising her hand.) I have a question. Why do some people call it a "chalkboard" and other people call it a "**blackboard**"?

Instructor: It really doesn't **make** any **difference** which word you use. We used to call them "blackboards" because they were made of black slate, a kind of hard rock. Now most of them are made of green plastic. We call them "chalkboards" because we write on them with chalk. Sometimes we just say "board."

    Student: Thank you. Sometimes English can be very confusing.

Questions

1. Where does the instructor tell the students to write the assignment?
2. Explain the meaning of **copy** in this dialogue.
3. Why were chalkboards formerly called "blackboards"?
4. What are most of these boards made of today?
5. What things do you find confusing about the English language?

6. **Instructor:** Please **hand in** your **homework** at the end of the class.

Student: Professor, I didn't know you were going to collect the assignment. I wrote the sentences in my notebook **by mistake**. Can I **copy** my homework **over** and hand it in on Wednesday?

Instructor: I'd rather you put it in my mailbox in the department office tomorrow. I'm planning to correct your papers and **hand** them **back** on Wednesday, so we can discuss the **errors**.

Student: OK. I'll leave my paper in your mailbox tomorrow morning.

Questions

1. What does the instructor ask the students to do with their homework?
2. What did one student do by mistake? Why?
3. What does this student ask permission to do?
4. What does the instructor ask the student to do?
5. Why is the instructor going to return the students' papers on Wednesday?
6. On what day of the week do you think the dialogue takes place? Why?

7. **A:** Can you give me the homework assignment for tomorrow?

B: Professor Watson gave it to us at the end of the class. Didn't you get it?

A: No. I was **daydreaming** and I didn't hear it.

B: Why didn't you ask her to repeat it?

A: Because I didn't want her to know I wasn't **paying attention**.

B: OK. I'll give it to you. It's Exercise A **at the bottom of** page 17, and B **at the top of** page 18 and . . .

A: Wait a minute. Got a pencil? Thanks. Wait till I **write** that **down**. OK. I've got that. **Go ahead**.

B: Exercise C **in the middle of** page 18. Choose ten words from the vocabulary list and use them in sentences. Write on every other line and **underline** the words.

A: OK. I've got it now. Thanks a lot.

B: Don't mention it.

Questions

1. Why doesn't **A** know what the assignment is?
2. Why didn't **A** ask the professor to repeat the assignment?
3. What does **A** ask **B** for? Why?
4. What impression do you have of **A** as a student?
5. How do you know that the professor is a woman?

8. **A:** How's your English class? Are you still **afraid** to speak?

B: No. Not so much anymore. I'm **getting used to** it. It seems easier every day.

A: You see? I told you. You know more English than you think you do. All you need is practice in speaking it.

B: I guess you're right. I **used to tremble** every time the professor **called on** me. Now I'm not so afraid anymore.

Questions

1. What does **B** mean by "I'm getting used to it"?
2. What does **A** say about **B**'s knowledge of English?
3. What does **used to** mean? What's another word for **tremble**?
4. Why do you think **B** used to tremble when the professor called on him (or her)? Does the student still feel that way?

9. **A:** I didn't go to class today. Did Professor Cohen say when he was going to hand back our compositions?

B: He handed them back today. I have to **do** mine **over**. He told us to write in ink and I wrote **in pencil**. I also had a lot of mistakes.

A: I'll probably have to do mine over, too. I'm sure I **made** a lot of **mistakes**. I forgot to **read** it **over** before I handed it in.

B: I read over my whole paper—carefully. I thought. Professor Cohen said we should **read** our papers **aloud** to someone else before we hand them in.

A: Hey, that's a good idea. Let's try it next time. If *we* find our mistakes, then *he* won't find them. Maybe we'll get better grades.

B: OK. Let's try it and see what happens.

Questions

1. When did Professor Cohen hand back the papers? (Use a pronoun in your answer.)
2. Why did **B** have to do the composition over?
3. What did **A** forget to do before handing in the composition?
4. What advice did the professor give the students?
5. Why does **A** think the professor's advice is a good idea?

10. **A:** Did you study the vocabulary list? I had to **look up** several words.

B: I **looked over** the list quickly, but I didn't look up any words. I don't have a dictionary yet.

A: You don't? How do you expect to improve your English if you don't use a dictionary? There are dictionaries in the **reference room** in the library, you know.

B: Don't worry. I'll pick one up at the bookstore in a day or two.

Questions

1. Did **B** study the vocabulary list carefully?
2. Why didn't **B** look up any words?
3. Where are there dictionaries that **B** can use?
4. What kind of books can be found in the reference room of a library?
5. When and where is **B** going to buy a dictionary?
6. Why is it important for every student to have a dictionary?

VOCABULARY

These words and expressions have been used in the dialogues and/or exercises in this lesson. You have probably been able to understand their meaning from the way they are used in this lesson. It is not necessary for you to memorize all of the items on the list, but you should be able to understand their meaning when you hear someone else use them.

DIALOGUE 1

index card
permanent address
local (temporary) address
row – seats, etc. arranged in a line
erase
print (v)
upper left-hand, right-hand (corner)
in ink
skip a line – write on every other line
pass to the right, left, front, back
pass out (S) – hand out, distribute

DIALOGUE 2

rollbook – classbook, class record
student number
handwriting – longhand, script
call the roll – take attendance

fill out (S)
come (came) in – enter
make (made) out (S) – able to read, see, hear

DIALOGUE 3

textbook
mistake – error
look on with
cross out (S) – draw a line through
make sure

DIALOGUE 4

parentheses
circle (the, a) word – draw a line around
raise (my, your, his, her) hand
take (took) out (S)

DIALOGUE 5

assignment, homework assignment
chalkboard, blackboard, board
notebook
make a difference
copy (v)

DIALOGUE 6

homework
error
by mistake
hand in (S)
hand back (S)
copy over (S)

DIALOGUE 7

daydream
at the bottom of
in the middle of
at the top of
underline – draw a line under
pay attention (to)

go ahead – continue
write (wrote) down (S)

DIALOGUE 8

tremble
(to be) afraid (of)
get used to – get accustomed to
used to – in the past but not now
call on

DIALOGUE 9

in pencil
make a mistake
do (did) over (S) – do again
read over (S)
read aloud (S)

DIALOGUE 10

reference room
look up (S)
look over (S)

QUESTIONS FOR CLASS DISCUSSION

> **NOTE TO INSTRUCTOR:** Choose only those questions appropriate to your particular class.

1. How many letters are there in the English alphabet?
2. Which letters in the English alphabet do you find the most difficult to remember?
3. What is the difference between alphabetical order and chronological order?
4. When you were in grade school and high school, did you have to buy your own textbooks or did the school provide them for you?
5. What were your favorite subjects in high school? Which subjects did you like least?
6. About how many students were there in each class when you went to high school?
7. About how many students do you think there should be in an English class?
8. Where do you prefer to sit in a classroom? In the first row or near the front? In the last row or near the back? In the middle (center) of the room?

9. Do you prefer to use one loose-leaf notebook for all your courses, or do you prefer to use a separate notebook for each course? What are the advantages and/or disadvantages of each system?

10. What are some of the things you used to like to do when you were younger (in high school, for instance) that no longer interest you?

11. Have you ever done the wrong assignment or made a mistake in something because you were daydreaming or not paying attention when the instructions were given? Tell the class about it briefly.

12. Have you ever lost points on an assignment or a test because you didn't follow the instructions? Tell the class about your experience.

HOMEWORK

Part I. Incomplete Dialogues

Complete these dialogues with the appropriate question or response, using words or expressions you have learned in this lesson. Make sure you refer to the vocabulary list. Be careful to use the correct word order in asking the questions (notice **1. A** and **4. A**, for example). *When a word or an expression has more than one meaning, use the meaning discussed in this lesson.*

1. **A:** What does the word **underline** mean?

    B: It means to _____ .

2. **A:** What _____ mean?

    B: It means to draw a line through a word.

3. **A:** What _____ mean?

    B: It means to write on every other line.

4. **A:** What does **hand out** mean?

    B: It means to _____ .

5. **A:** Did you _____ your homework assignment today?
                         (separable verb)

    B: Not yet. I have to _____ it _____ .
    (There are two possible answers.)

Part II. Vocabulary Building

Review the dialogues carefully. Then use each of the following expressions in a sentence of your own. In the sentence you write, be sure that the meaning of the expression will be clear to the reader. Underline the expressions. *When an expression has more than one meaning, use the meaning discussed in this lesson.* Of course, you may use additional vocabulary items from this lesson or from Lesson 1.

make a difference

pay attention (to)

get used to

used to – formerly, in the past but not now

in ink, in pencil *(choose one)*

make a mistake

look up (S)

fill out (S)

look on with

make out (S)

LISTENING COMPREHENSION EXERCISE: STUDENT'S ANSWER SHEET

1. ____a) draw a line under it.

    ____b) draw a line around it.

    ____c) draw a line through it.

2. ____a) answer a question orally.

    ____b) write in his notebook.

    ____c) speak on the telephone.

3. ____a) write it again on another piece of paper.

    ____b) make changes in what she has written.

    ____c) look at another student's assignment.

4. ____a) do it again correctly.

    ____b) make an exact copy.

    ____c) write on the other side of the paper.

5. ____a) use a dictionary.

    ____b) review what he has written.

    ____c) get more information.

6. ____a) draw a line through it.

    ____b) draw a line around it.

    ____c) draw a line under it.

7. ____a) ask for some bread.

    ____b) take attendance.

    ____c) act in a play.

8. ____**a)** still collects them.

____**b)** collected them in the past but not now.

____**c)** is accustomed to collecting them.

9. ____**a)** listen carefully.

____**b)** attend the class.

____**c)** give some money.

10. ____**a)** He likes getting up early now.

____**b)** He doesn't get up early anymore.

____**c)** He's accustomed to getting up early now.

CONVERSATION PRACTICE

With a classmate, choose one of the following situations and make up a dialogue using appropriate words and expressions from the vocabulary list for this lesson. Then, according to your instructor's directions, present your dialogue to the rest of the class. Each person should speak at least twice.

1. A professor (Student **A**) is explaining an assignment and one of the students (Student **B**) asks a question about the meaning of something the professor says. The professor explains what the student asks about and the student makes an appropriate reply.

2. At the end of the class, Student **A** asks Student **B** for the assignment for the next class because he was not paying attention and did not hear what the professor assigned. Student **B** explains the assignment and Student **A** responds appropriately.

3. Student **A** does not have a textbook. He explains why to the student sitting next to him (Student **B**) and asks Student **B** to share the book for this class.

4. The professor (Student **A**) has just finished calling the roll and your name (Student **B**) was not mentioned. Raise your hand and explain the situation to the professor, who responds accordingly.

5. You (Student **A**) arrived late the first day of class and today you discover that the professor (Student **B**) does not have your name in his rollbook. You explain what happened and the professor responds appropriately.

6. You (Student **A**) did your homework assignment but you aren't satisfied with the appearance of it. You ask permission to copy it over and hand it in at the next class session. The professor (Student **B**) gives his or her permission and you respond appropriately.

7. The professor (Student **A**) cannot read what you (Student **B**) have written as your family name and asks you to spell it. He or she also asks you for your student number.

8. You (Student **A**) ask the student next to you (Student **B**) his or her name because you have forgotten it. You do not know how to write his or her last name so you ask the student to spell it. Student **B** obliges and you (Student **A**) repeat the name as it has been spelled.

9. You (Student **A**) handed in your homework during the previous class, but the professor (Student **B**) has just returned it to you, saying that you did not follow instructions. (You and your partner decide what these instructions were.) You ask permission to do the assignment again, and the professor responds appropriately.

10. With another classmate, make up a situation of your own in which you use words and expressions from the vocabulary list.

3

Let's Talk About Time: Telling Time, Discussing Schedules and Routines

DIALOGUES

In studying these dialogues, pay careful attention to boldface vocabulary items. You should be able to learn their meanings from the way in which they are used in the various dialogues. Practice reading the dialogues aloud with a classmate. Answer the questions after each dialogue.

1. **A:** You're **yawning** and you look **exhausted**! Didn't you get enough sleep last night?

B: Sorry (yawning). Excuse the **yawn**. I didn't **get to bed** until after twelve o'clock and I got up at 5:30.

A: 5:30? That's like the middle of the night for me. Why did you **get up** so early?

B: Well, I had to make the kids' lunches and **get** them **ready** for school before I **left for** work. It's always such a rush. And then, at the last minute, I had to iron a shirt.

A: Couldn't you fix the lunches and **get** your clothes **ready** the night before?

B: Yeah, I suppose I could. But by the time I **do the dishes** and **put** the kids **to bed** I'm **dead tired**. All I feel like doing is **stretching out** in front of the TV. Last night I **stayed up** to watch the end of a dumb movie. This morning I'm so **sleepy** I can hardly keep my eyes open.

> **NOTE:** The word **watch** means to observe something or someone carefully for a certain amount of time. *For example:* Please **watch** the children for a few minutes while I go to the store. We **watch** the six o'clock news broadcast every night on TV.
>
> The word **look** means to direct one's eyes in order to see someone or something in particular. **Look** is often used with the word **at**. *For example:* **Look**! There's your friend coming now. **Look** at this picture.
>
> The word **see**, means, among other things, to get knowledge through the eyes. *For example:* I can **see** the ocean from my window.

Questions

1. What's another way of saying "after twelve o'clock" in this dialogue?
2. How do you know **B**'s children are young?
3. Do you think **B** is a man or a woman? Why?
4. Do you think **B** is married or divorced? What gives you that impression?
5. What's another way of saying "do the dishes"?
6. How do you know **B** didn't like the movie?

7. Was **B** sitting up or lying down while watching TV? Why do you think so?

8. Where do you think **A** and **B** are having their conversation? What makes you think so?

9. What kind of relationship is there between **A** and **B**? Explain your answer.

2. **A:** You were **absent from** English class this morning? **How come?**

B: (*A male student*) I **overslept**. I set the alarm but forgot to **wind the clock** and it **ran down**. I **woke up** too late to make my eight o'clock class.

A: You mean you're still using a **wind-up alarm clock**? Why don't you get an electric clock?

B: I used to have one, but you can't depend on that either. Sometimes the electricity **goes off** for a while during the night and then I'm late for class anyway.

A: I **set the alarm** on my **digital watch**. It's very dependable. Maybe you should try that.

B: I did. The alarm isn't loud enough. When it **goes off**, I don't even hear it. I sleep right through it. I just can't win. I don't know what the answer is because I really don't like to get up early.

Questions

1. Why was **B** absent from his eight o'clock class?

2. What is the difference in meaning of **make** in the expressions "make the kids' lunch" in Dialogue 1 and "make my eight o'clock class" in Dialogue 2?

3. What's the difference in meaning between the expressions **the electricity goes off** and **the alarm goes off**?

4. Why would the electricity going off for a while cause **B** to be late for class?

5. Why can't **B** use the alarm on his wristwatch to wake him up?

6. To what is **B** referring when he says "I just can't win"?

7. What suggestion would you make to **B** to help him get up on time?

8. What is the relationship between the two speakers? How can you tell?

3. **A:** What's the matter? You look **down** this morning. Is something bothering you?

B: Nothing's the matter. I'm just so tired of the same old routine—doing the same things day after day, week after week, month after month. I'm **in a rut**. I need a vacation—or some time off to do something different for a change.

A: I have an idea! Business is slow right now. Why don't you **take** a week **off** to relax and **take it easy**? Does your daughter still have her place up in the country?

B: Yes, she does. As a matter of fact, she keeps asking me to come up and **spend** some **time** with her. I'll **take** her **up on** it next week. That fresh clear mountain air will **do** me **good**. I can rest and **catch up on** my sleep. I can stay in bed as late as I want to and not have to **worry about keeping** a **schedule**.

A: Sounds great! I wish I could go with you.

B: Why don't you come up on the bus next Saturday and **stay over**? I know Betty'll be glad to see you. She always asks me how you're doing. We can **drive back** together on Sunday night.

A: Thanks for the invitation. I just may do that if I can get somebody to **stay with** the children. I'll let you know during the week.

B: OK. Just give me a call. The number is 362-7405—same area code.

Questions

1. What does **A** mean by "you look down"?
2. Why does **B** say, "I'm in a rut"?
3. Why do you think **A** says "up in the country" rather than just "in the country"? (See **B**'s answer.)
4. How do you know the two people work together?
5. What is the relationship between **A** and **B**? How do you know?
6. What's another way of saying "stay with the children"?
7. Who is older — **A** or **B**? How do you know? Are they women or men? Why do you think so?

4. A: What are you doing up so early and where are you **dashing out** to in such a hurry?

B: To the university. Where else? I'm **in a** big **rush** because the professor gets very **upset** if we don't come to class **on time**.

A: But it's Saturday! You don't have classes on Saturday!

B: Saturday! It's Saturday? I'm **going back** to bed. Wake me up at twelve o'clock.

A: You see—that's what happens when you **stay out** so late. The next morning you're so **groggy** you don't even know what day it is.

Questions

1. Who do you think **A** is? Why?
2. What does "in a rush" mean? Why is **B** in a rush?
3. What does **B** mean by "the professor gets very upset"?
4. What's the meaning of **on time** in this dialogue?
5. What's another way of saying "twelve o'clock" in this dialogue?
6. What do you think the word **groggy** means in this dialogue?

An Informal Way of Asking for the Time

5. A: What time is it, Kathy? My watch has stopped.

B: It's about 3:15. I just **glanced at** the kitchen clock a minute ago.

A: 3:15! We'd better **hurry up** and get ready. The plane leaves at 5:30.

B: What are you worried about? Take your time. That's two hours from now.

A: But what if we get caught in the **rush hour** traffic? We'll never get to the airport **in time*** and we'll **miss** the plane.

B: OK. If it'll make you feel better we'll leave in a few minutes. We'll get there in plenty of time.*

Questions

1. What are two other ways of saying "3:15"?

2. What's the meaning of **glance at** in this dialogue?

3. What's another way of saying "5:30"?

4. What's another way of saying "take your time"?

5. Why do you think **A** is worried about getting caught in rush-hour traffic? (In other words, how is rush-hour traffic different from ordinary traffic?)

6. What does **A** mean by "we'll miss the plane"?

7. Where are the people who are speaking? How do you know?

A More Polite Way of Asking for the Time

6. A: Do you have the time, please?

B: Certainly. I'm not sure, but I think it's about a quarter to three. My watch has been **running fast**. It **gains** several minutes a day.

A: Mine's just the opposite. It's slow—it loses about thirty minutes a day. I don't know what's wrong with it. It used to **keep good time**.

B: Sounds as if we'd both better **get** our watches **fixed**.

A: Yeah, but I don't know what I'd do without my wristwatch. I'd be lost without it.

B: You could always **turn on** the radio or watch television to find out the time—or buy another watch.

Questions

1. What are two other ways of saying "a quarter to three"?

2. What's another way of saying "thirty minutes"?

3. What do we mean when we say that a watch **keeps good time**?

4. Why do you think **A**'s and **B**'s watches aren't keeping good time?

5. What does **A** mean by "I'd be lost without it"?

6. Which of **B**'s suggestions for **A** do you think is better? Why do you think so?

---

* When **in time** appears in a negative sentence, it means *too late*. When **in time** (**in** plenty of **time**) is used in an affirmative sentence, it means *early* or *ahead of time*.

7. What's another way of saying "get (something) fixed"?

8. Compare the request for the time in this dialogue with the request in Dialogue 5. How do they differ?

A Very Informal Way of Asking for the Time

7. **A:** What time is it, anyway?

B: Sorry, I don't have a watch. The class is supposed to end at 4:50. It must be about that time now.

A: I sure hope so. (Stretching and yawning.) It's so hot in here I'm **falling asleep**.

B: You're not the only one. I'm so **drowsy** I can hardly **stay awake**.

A: This is the last time I **sign up for** a late afternoon class in the summer.

B: Me too. All I'm **thinking about** now is going home, **lying down** on the bed, and listening to some cool jazz.

A: Not me. As soon as this class **lets out**, I'm going to go home and **take a nap** till dinner time.

Questions

1. What's another way of saying "4:50"?

2. How do you know neither **A** nor **B** is paying attention to the instructor?

3. How do you know the classroom isn't air-conditioned?

4. Who do you think is sleepier — **A** or **B**? What makes you think so?

5. What's another way of saying "take a nap"?

6. What's another way of saying "lets out"?

VOCABULARY

Some of the most frequently used words and expressions in English are those dealing with time. In this lesson, we have concentrated on these most important vocabulary items. However, in the dialogues we have included some other frequently used words and expressions which do not have to do with time. As you look over the list on the next page you will find that you already know the meanings of most of the words from the way they have been used in the various dialogues. While it is not necessary for you to be able to use all of these words and expressions, you should be able to recognize them and know their meanings when you see them in print or hear them used by another speaker.

DIALOGUE 1

yawn (n *and* v)
exhausted – dead tired
sleepy
do (did) the dishes
get (got) to bed – go to bed
get up (S)
get ready (S)
leave (left) for
put —— to bed (S)
stretch out (S)
stay up

DIALOGUE 2

wind-up clock, alarm clock
digital watch
absent from
how come?
oversleep
set the alarm
wind (wound) the clock
run (ran) down – stop operating or
    running due to lack of power
wake (woke, waked) up (S)
go (went) off – stop functioning
go off – ring, make a loud sound

DIALOGUE 3

down (adj.)
be in a rut
keep (kept) a schedule
spend time
take it easy
do —— good (S)
catch (caught) up on
worry about
stay over
stay with
drive (drove) back (S)
take —— off (S)
take —— up on (S)

DIALOGUE 4

on time
groggy
dash out
stay out
(be) in a rush
(be, get) upset
go back

DIALOGUE 5

rush hour
in time
glance at
hurry up
miss (a bus, plane, train)

DIALOGUE 6

run fast
gain – go faster
keep good time
turn on (S)
get —— fixed (S)

DIALOGUE 7

fall (fell) asleep
take (took) a nap
stay awake
drowsy
sign up for
lie (lay) down
think about
let out (S)

VOCABULARY STUDY: TELLING TIME

Study these drawings and learn the vocabulary related to telling time. Many of the expressions you probably already know. Concentrate on those you don't know so that you will be able to use them and/or recognize them when they are used by another speaker.

1.

counter-clockwise   clockwise

a. hour hand
b. minute hand
c. second hand
d. alarm

The face of the clock

2. Minutes on side B of the clock face are expressed by the words *of, to, till* or *before* the hour. *Past* and *after* are also used, as in "forty-five minutes after one."

Minutes on side A of the clock are expressed with the words *after* or *past* the hour.

3.

a) five o'clock
b) five sharp
c) exactly five
d) on the dot

4.

a) five-ten
b) ten (minutes) past five
c) ten (minutes) after five

5.

a) five-fifteen
b) fifteen (minutes) past five
c) fifteen (minutes) after five
d) (a) quarter past five
e) (a) quarter after five

6.

a) five-thirty
b) half-past five
c) thirty minutes past five*
d) thirty minutes after five*

7.

a) five-forty
b) twenty (minutes) of six
c) twenty (minutes) to six
d) twenty (minutes) till six
e) twenty (minutes) before six

8.

a) five forty-five
b) (a) quarter to six
c) (a) quarter of six
d) (a) quarter before six
e) (a) quarter till six
f) fifteen (minutes) to six
g) fifteen (minutes) of six
h) fifteen (minutes) until six
i) fifteen (minutes) before six

_____
* Used by radio announcers

36

9.

  a) twelve o'clock
  b) twelve noon (PM)
  c) twelve midnight (AM)

> **NOTE:** **1-1/2 hours** is read "one and a half hours." An alternate is "an hour and a half." The letter *h* is not pronounced in **hour**, but it is pronounced in the word **half**. The *l* in **half** is silent.

QUESTIONS FOR CLASS DISCUSSION

1. Do you get up at the same time every day during the week? What time is that? How about on weekends?

2. (At) what time do you usually go to bed on weekdays? On weekends?

3. Have you ever missed an important appointment, test, etc. because you overslept? What were the consequences? Tell the class about it briefly.

4. What do you do when you wake up in the middle of the night and you can't sleep?

5. Have you ever jumped out of bed in a hurry and then realized it was Saturday and you didn't have to get up early? What did you do — go back to bed or get up?

6. What's the first thing you do when you get out of bed in the morning?

7. What's the last thing you do before you turn out the light and go to bed at night?

8. Do you follow the same routine every day or does your schedule vary from day to day?

9. For what sort of an event or occasion would you stay out late on a weekday?

10. Have you ever stayed up all night? What was the reason?

11. What's the latest you've ever slept after staying out late the night before?

12. What are some of the things you have to do after you get out of class or work?

13. Do you often take a nap in the afternoon? About how long do you sleep?

14. Do you ever lie down and listen to music to relax after you've finished your work? What sort of music do you prefer for this purpose?

15. What are some of the things you like to do to relax after a busy day?

16. How do you like to spend a long weekend? In other words, what are some of the things you might do?

HOMEWORK

Part I. Vocabulary Building

Following your instructor's directions, use some or all of these expressions and two-word verbs in dialogues or sentences of your own. Be sure that their meanings are clear in what you write. *If a word or expression has more than one meaning, choose the meaning used in this lesson.* Write some of your dialogues or sentences in the past tense.

do the dishes	miss (a plane)
wind the clock (*or* alarm clock)	on time
set the alarm	go off – ring, make a loud sound
keep a schedule	run down – stop operating
fall asleep	stay up
oversleep	stay out
in time	stay over
in a rush *or* in a hurry (*choose one*)	lie down
spend time	worry about
yawn	take time (a day, a week, etc.) off (S)

Part II. Telling Time

Use as many phrases as you can to express the time shown on each of the clocks below.

_____   _____   _____

_____   _____

_____

_____   _____   _____

_____   _____   _____

                                                _____

LISTENING COMPREHENSION EXERCISE: STUDENT'S ANSWER SHEET

Part I

1.

2.

3.

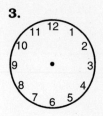

4.

5.

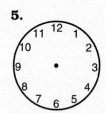

Part II

1. _____ **a)** He looked at it quickly.

_____ **b)** He looked at it carefully.

_____ **c)** He looked at it for a long time.

2. _____ **a)** He slept at a friend's house.

_____ **b)** He slept longer than he had planned to sleep.

_____ **c)** He slept badly.

3. _____ **a)** take care of the children.

_____ **b)** take the children to her house.

_____ **c)** visit the children.

4. ___ **a)** It rings or makes a loud sound.

___ **b)** It explodes.

___ **c)** It stops functioning.

5. ___ **a)** He's going to sleep for a short time.

___ **b)** He's going to eat something.

___ **c)** He's going for a walk.

CONVERSATION PRACTICE

With another student, choose one of the following situations and make up a dialogue using appropriate words and expressions from the vocabulary items used in this lesson. Limit your dialogue to three or four exchanges (**A B, A B, A B, A B**). After you have practiced your dialogue, present it to the class according to your instructor's directions.

1. **A** has an appointment in another part of the city at a certain hour. (You decide the time and the nature of the appointment.) **B** has offered to drive **A** to the appointment. Because of the time of day, **A** is worrying about being late. **B** tells **A** that there is plenty of time but to please **A**, **B** agrees to leave earlier than he or she has planned to.

2. **A** notices that a co-worker, **B**, looks tired this morning. **A** is concerned and starts a conversation to find out what **B**'s problem is and tries to be helpful in finding a solution to the problem.

3. Student **A** noticed that Student **B** was absent from an earlier class. **A** finds out that **B** overslept and they discuss the problem.

4. You have seen from the dialogues in this lesson that asking someone for the time is a good way of starting a conversation. Using *one* of the expressions below, begin a conversation with another student according to your instructor's directions. Limit your dialogue to three exchanges: **A B, A B, A B,** ending with an appropriate expression.

   What time is it, _____ ?

   Do you have the time, please?

   Can (Could) you please tell me the time?

   What time does your watch say?

4

Let's Talk About Studying and Taking Examinations

DIALOGUES

As you study these dialogues, notice how the boldface vocabulary items are used. Then answer the questions relating to each dialogue. Practice reading the dialogues aloud, preferably with another person.

1. **A:** Do you have any idea what the **midterm exam** will be like?

   B: No, I don't. Not the slightest. But I hope it's all **short-answer, fill-in**-the-blank-type questions. I **do** much **better** on that kind of exam.

   A: I don't like **multiple-choice** questions, myself. Sometimes I think more than one answer can be correct. Then I have trouble choosing only one. I **end up** guessing. Sometimes I guess right and sometimes I don't. That's why I prefer **essay exams**.

   B: Yeah, but with essay questions I have a problem organizing my thoughts. It takes me so long to write the answer that sometimes I **run out of** time. I have to **turn in** my paper before I'm finished.

   A: Have you ever tried **jotting down** all your ideas on a piece of **scrap paper** first? Before you start writing your answer? That's what works for me.

   B: Hey, that sounds like a good idea. I think I'll try it next time I have an essay exam. Maybe I'll do better.

Questions

1. During what part of a semester would a midterm examination be given?
2. Why does **A** dislike multiple-choice questions?
3. What does "I end up guessing" mean?
4. What's another way of saying "jot down your ideas"?
5. What is scrap paper?
6. What's another way of saying "I'll do better"?

2. **A:** Hey, Bill, where are you rushing in such a hurry?

   B: Over to the lecture hall. I want to get there in time to get a front seat. Last week when we had that guest **lecturer** I sat toward the back. I could hardly hear because of all the traffic noise outside. I hardly **took** any **notes** on the **lecture**.

   A: I took quite a few notes. Why don't you **come over** tonight? We can **look through** them, and you can copy whatever you need. It'll give me a chance to **brush up on** what I **took down**.

   B: OK. I'll **stop by** on my way home from work.

   A: Say, as long as you're going to the library, could you **drop off** this book for me? I **took** it **out** last night on overnight reserve. It's due at four o'clock. If you **take** it **back** for me it'll save me a trip. →

B: Sure. Give it to me. **I'm due** there at three o'clock. I'll see you tonight about eight o'clock. OK?

A: OK. Fine. I'll see you then.

Questions

1. Why does **A** want to get a seat in the front row?
2. What does the expression **brush up on** mean here?
3. How do you know that **B** works in the library?
4. What does **drop off** mean in this dialogue?
5. What does **B** mean by "I'm due there at 3:00"?

3. **A:** Hi, Jane. How're you doing this semester? I haven't seen you since **registration**.

B: Not very well. I **got off to a bad start**. I was sick for two weeks at the beginning of the semester. I'm thinking of **dropping out** till next fall.

A: Dropping out? Are you serious? If you leave before the end of the semester, you'll lose all the money you paid for **tuition**.

B: I know. But I don't want to take the chance of **flunking** a couple of courses. It would ruin my **average**. I'm planning to get a job and **earn** the money for next fall's tuition.

A: I still think you shouldn't drop out. Why don't you speak to your professors? Maybe you could **make up** the work you missed when you were sick. Or maybe you could ask a couple of them to give you an **incomplete**.

B: Maybe I'll do that. I really don't want to drop out. I'll **talk** it **over** with some of my professors and see what they think.

Questions

1. At what time of the year does this conversation take place? How do you know?
2. Why does **B** want to drop out? Why does **A** think that is a bad idea?
3. What is the meaning of **average** in this dialogue?
4. What is the meaning of the word **tuition**?
5. What's another way of saying "flunk a course"?
6. What's the meaning of the expression **an incomplete**?

4. **A:** Hey, Tom, where've you been? Haven't seen you in a while. Have you been sick?

B: N-a-ah. I've just been **cutting classes** a lot. I had a personal problem I had to **work out**. I'm **looking for** Professor Jordan. Do you know if he's **come in** yet?

A: He'll probably be here in a few minutes. It's still early. Say, did you hear what happened to your friend Sal? He **got caught cheating** on a test.

B: Yeah. I heard the teacher **tore up** his paper and gave him an **F** on the test.

I guess that means he'll **fail the course**, but that's his problem. Excuse me, here comes Professor Jordan. I have to speak to him. Excuse me, Professor Jordan. May I speak to you for a minute?

C: Certainly, Tom. I've been wondering what happened to you. You've **missed** so many classes.

B: That's what I want to talk to you about. I had a personal problem I had to solve, and I couldn't come to your class. I'd like to **drop** the **course**. I need your **signature** on this **drop card**. Would you please **sign** it for me?

C: Of course. You know this is the last day you can drop.

B: I know. **I put off** coming to see you until **the last minute**. I really don't want to drop because I enjoy the class a lot. But right now, I just don't have enough time to study for it.

C: I see. Well, in that case I think you've made the right decision. Good luck to you.

B: Thank you, sir.

Questions

1. What's another way of saying "I've been cutting classes"? How do you know that Tom has been cutting other classes besides Professor Jordan's?

2. What does the expression **work out** mean in this dialogue?

3. What do you think Sal might have been doing when the teacher saw him cheating?

4. What kind of personal problem might Tom have had?

5. What's a synonym for **put off** as it is used in this dialogue?

6. What does the expression **the last minute** mean?

5. A: How's your final exam schedule? I have three **in a row**, one right after the other next week.

B: Mine's not bad. But I'll sure be glad to **get** them **over with**. It's been a **tough** semester for me. Are you planning to go to summer school?

A: I was hoping to **take** some **time out** for a vacation or maybe get a part-time job. But I just found out I have to take an **undergraduate** physics course. It's a **prerequisite** for a **graduate course** I plan to take in the fall. How about you?

B: I dropped a math course this semester. I want to take it again this summer so I can graduate next December.

A: Then I'll probably see you around. **In the meantime**, good luck on your exams.

B: Thanks. You, too. What're you doing during the **break** after exams?

A: Nothing much. Just **resting up**—relaxing. You know, taking it easy. Taking that physics course during the summer is going to be **rough**.

B: Yeah, I know what you mean. The only good thing about the summer session is that it goes fast.

Questions

1. When do you think this conversation takes place? How do you know?
2. Can you think of some reasons why **B** says it was a tough semester?
3. What is a prerequisite?
4. What year of college is **B** in? How do you know?
5. What's the meaning of **break** in this dialogue?
6. What does **rough** mean as it is used here?
7. How can you tell that neither **A** nor **B** is going to enjoy going to summer school?

6. A: You know what happened to me last night? I was studying in the library. I was so tired I **put** my head **down** on the table to rest. I **dozed off** and I started to **snore**—and you know how quiet that place is!

B: Yeah. It's like a tomb. So what happened? Did somebody wake you up?

A: The guy next to me. But everybody was laughing. I've never been so embarrassed in my life. I wanted to **crawl** into a hole and disappear.

B: Did the guy **in charge throw** you **out** for making too much noise?

A: No. **Actually**, he was very nice. He was laughing too. He just told me I'd better get some sleep. So I put my **stuff** together and left.

B: That's why I always study in my room. If I fall asleep and start to snore, nobody knows it but me.

Questions

1. What's another way of saying "I dozed off"?
2. Why was **A** so embarrassed? If you had been **A** would you have been embarrassed?
3. What's another word that means the same as **actually**?
4. How do you know that the person in charge in the library was not angry with **A**?
5. What does **A** mean by "I put my stuff together"?
6. Do you ever fall asleep while you are studying?
7. Have you ever fallen asleep in a class? What happened?

7. A: How do you think you **made out** on the final exam?

B: Pretty well, I think. **For once** I did most of the required reading, and my notes were pretty **up-to-date**, for a change. How about you?

A: Pretty bad. I'm worried. I stayed up practically all night **cramming**. This morning I was so tired I couldn't **think straight**. I couldn't understand the first question. By the time I **figured** it **out**, I had **used up** too much time.

B: Well, were you able to finish? It was a pretty long exam.

A: No, I had to **leave out** the whole last question. I ran out of time. I sure hope

Mr. Jackson **marks on the curve**.* If he does, I may get a **passing grade**. If he doesn't, I've had it.

B: Don't worry. You probably did better than you think. Besides, even if you flunk the exam, you can still **pass the course**. Class participation counts, and you're pretty good at that.

A: Yeah, well, keep your fingers crossed for me. See you later.

B: Will do. Forget about the exam and enjoy the weekend.

Questions

1. How do you know that **B** doesn't always keep up with his or her classwork?
2. Who do you think is the better student—**A** or **B**? Why?
3. What does the word **cram** mean in this dialogue?
4. Do you know what the expression **mark on the curve** means? Explain it to the class.
5. What does **A** mean by "I've had it"?
6. What's the opposite of a **passing grade**?
7. What encouragement does **B** offer **A**?
8. The word **pretty** has been used four times. Is the meaning the same in each case? Explain your answer.

8. **A:** Before I pass out the examinations and the **bluebooks**, are there any questions? No? OK. Inside the **booklet** you'll find several **sheets of** scrap **paper** to **make notes**. When you turn in your exam, tear up the scrap paper and **throw** it **away**. It's a three-hour exam, so you must finish by four o'clock.

B: Do we have to turn in the scrap paper with our exam?

A: No. I said to **throw** it **away**—in the wastebasket right here beside the desk.

B: Sorry, I didn't hear you. If we need another bluebook what do we do?

A: You just walk up to the desk and get one.

B: Thanks.

Questions

1. How do you know that **B** wasn't paying attention to the instructions?
2. Do you think **A** (the examination proctor) is a professor or a student assistant? What makes you think so?
3. Why do you think the booklet used for writing answers to examinations is called a "bluebook"? How is a booklet different from a book?

---

* The expression "grades on the curve" is also used.

4. Since the proctor is passing out scrap paper and bluebooks, what type of examination do you think is being given?

5. What's the difference in meaning between these two expressions: **take notes** and **make notes**?

6. What time is it when the examination begins?

7. What's a synonym for **turn in** in this dialogue? (Refer to Lesson 2, Dialogue 6.)

VOCABULARY

The following words and expressions have been used in the dialogues and exercises of this lesson. You have probably figured out the meaning of most of these vocabulary items from the way in which they are used in the dialogues. Review the dialogues and study the vocabulary items listed for each dialogue.

DIALOGUE 1

midterm exam
short-answer (test)
multiple-choice
essay exam
scrap paper
fill in (S)
end up
run out of (S)
turn in (S)
jot down (S)

DIALOGUE 2

lecture (n)
lecturer
take notes
(be) due – expected or scheduled to be
come over
look through
brush up on
take (took) down (S)
stop by
drop off (S)
take out (S) – borrow (as a book from a library)
take back (S)

DIALOGUE 3

registration
tuition
an incomplete (grade)
average – academic standing
earn
talk over (S)
get (got) off to a bad start
flunk (fail) a course
drop out (of)
make up (S)

DIALOGUE 4

cut class
get caught
cheat (v)
drop card
drop a course
fail a course
miss – be absent from
the last minute
sign (v)
signature
work out (S)
look for
come in – arrive
tear (tore) up (S)
put off (S)

DIALOGUE 5

undergraduate course
graduate course
prerequisite
break (n)
rough – tough, very difficult
in a row – one after the other
take time out
in the meantime
rest up
get over with (S)

DIALOGUE 6

snore (v)
crawl (v)
actually
stuff (n)
(be) in charge
put down (S)
doze off
throw (threw) out (S)

DIALOGUE 7

cram
think straight
mark on a curve
passing grade
pass a course
for once
up-to-date
figure out (S)
use up (S)
make out – manage to do
leave (left) out (S)

DIALOGUE 8

bluebook
booklet
sheet of paper
make notes
throw (threw) away (S)

QUESTIONS FOR CLASS DISCUSSION

> **NOTE TO INSTRUCTOR:** Select only those questions which are appropriate for your particular class according to the amount of class time you plan to allow for the activity.

1. Where do you prefer to study? In the library? In your room? In another place? Why?

2. Do you usually study alone or with a friend (or friends)?

3. What do you think about study groups?

4. Does noise (traffic, TV or radio, people talking) bother you when you're trying to study?

5. Do you listen to music while you study? If so, what kind do you prefer?

6. Do you like to eat or nibble on something or drink something while you study?

7. When you have an exam the next day, do you prefer to finish studying the night before, or early in the morning on the day of the exam?

8. Have you ever stayed up all night cramming for an exam? What was the result?

9. About how many hours (days) do you usually study for a final exam?

10. Which kind of examination do you prefer: the fill-in-the-blank, short-answer type; the multiple-choice type; the essay type; or a combination? Why?

11. Do you have any particular strategy for handling an examination? That is, do you answer the easiest questions first or do you take the more difficult ones and leave the easy ones till the last? Explain your answer.

12. How do you budget your time during an examination?

13. When you are taking an essay examination, do you use scrap paper to organize your thoughts, or do you begin writing the answers immediately?

14. How do you feel about being asked to write a term paper instead of taking an examination?

15. How do you feel about a series of tests throughout the semester as opposed to a midterm and final examination?

16. About how much do you think a student's class participation should count towards the final grade for a course?

17. Do you think that all members of a class, even those with an *A* average, should be required to take the final examination?

18. Which class format do you prefer — lecture or class discussion?

19. In your culture, how is a student who is caught cheating penalized?

20. Do you have a habit of putting off doing unpleasant things until the last minute? Give an example.

HOMEWORK

Part I. Using Two-Word Verbs

These dialogues contain words or expressions similar in meaning to the two-word verbs listed below. In the space provided, write the two-word verb which is closest in meaning to the boldface portion of the statement. Use the past tense where necessary.

figure out	come over	jot down
talk over	leave out	brush up on
drop off	doze off	tear up
make out	use up	take back

Example: A: When are you going to **return** these books to the library?

B: I'll _____ them _____ at the end of the week.

1. **A:** Have you **reviewed** all the material for the final exam yet?

   B: Not yet. I plan to _____ everything in the next few days.

2. **A:** The exam was very long. Did you have to **omit** any of the questions?

   B: As a matter of fact, I _____ the last question.

3. **A:** Are you going to **discuss** your problem with your mathematics professor?

   B: I'm planning to _____ it _____ with him tomorrow.

4. **A:** Why don't you **visit** me tonight and we'll study together?

   B: OK. I'll _____ _____ after dinner.

5. **A:** I couldn't **understand** what the professor wanted us to do for the assignment.

   B: At first I couldn't either, but I finally _____ it _____ .

6. **A:** Why did you **destroy** the term paper you were working on?

   B: I _____ it _____ because I decided to write about a different topic.

7. **A:** You **slept** during the last part of the TV show.

   B: I know. I _____ _____ and I missed the ending.

8. **A:** Please **write** my address in your address book.

   B: I don't have my address book here. I'll _____ it _____ on this piece of paper.

9. **A:** Do you think Bill will **be successful** in his new job?

   B: Of course. He'll _____ _____ very well because he's well-prepared.

10. **A:** Don't forget to **leave** your blue suit at the dry cleaners.

    B: I won't. I'll _____ it _____ on my way to work.

Part II. Vocabulary Building

Use the following expressions and two-word verbs in dialogues or sentences of your own. You may want to use additional vocabulary items from the various dialogues. Use the past tense in some of your sentences or dialogues.

registration

tuition

prerequisite

lecturer *or* lecture *(choose one)*

take time out

get off to a bad start

fail a course *or* pass a course

   (choose one)

get (something) over with (S)

drop out (of)

run out of

turn in (S)

make up (S)

rest up

take out (S)

put off (S)

LISTENING COMPREHENSION EXERCISE: STUDENT'S ANSWER SHEET

Part I

1. ____ **a)** listen to it.

____ **b)** write it.

____ **c)** look for it.

2. ____ **a)** review them.

____ **b)** write them again.

____ **c)** look for them.

3. ____ **a)** wants to be there.

____ **b)** is scheduled to be there.

____ **c)** can be there.

4. ____ **a)** discussed his plans.

____ **b)** disagreed about his plans.

____ **c)** decided on his plans.

5. ____ **a)** I went to class.

____ **b)** I taught class.

____ **c)** I was absent from class.

Part II

1. ____ **a)** let the suit fall to the floor.

____ **b)** left it.

____ **c)** picked it up.

2. ____ **a)** removing it.

    ____ **b)** writing it.

    ____ **c)** reading it.

3. ____ **a)** added a sentence.

    ____ **b)** underlined a sentence.

    ____ **c)** omitted a sentence.

4. ____ **a)** borrow a book.

    ____ **b)** return a book.

    ____ **c)** buy a book.

5. ____ **a)** do the arithmetic for it.

    ____ **b)** remember the answer to it.

    ____ **c)** understand it.

CONVERSATION PRACTICE

Below are some situations. With another student, make up a dialogue for one of the situations using vocabulary items from this lesson. Present your dialogue to the class according to your instructor's directions. Use the **A B, A B, A B** form for your dialogue; that is, each person speaks three times.

1. Two friends are discussing a recent examination in a certain subject. One of them thinks he or she did very well, but the other feels that he or she did very poorly. They talk about the reasons for their success or failure.

2. Two friends are comparing their study habits and find that they have very different ideas about how to study.

3. Two students attended a lecture. One of them sat in the back of the lecture hall and couldn't hear the speaker very well because there was noise outside. They meet the next day and the student who couldn't hear the lecturer complains that he or she couldn't take good notes. The other student has taken good notes and offers to share them. They arrange to meet later that day.

4. It's the end of the spring semester. Two students ask each other about their plans for the summer and discover that they both plan to go to summer school but for different reasons. They express their feelings about having to take summer classes.

5. Using the dialogues in this lesson as a guide, think up a situation of your own and make up a dialogue.

5

Let's Talk About
the Family

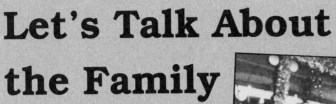

REFERENCE LIST OF FAMILY RELATIONSHIPS — THE FAMILY TREE

You will probably never have the occasion to use all of the items in the following list, but you should familiarize yourself with those you don't already know so that when you read them or when another speaker uses them, you will understand. Many of the items appear in the various dialogues of this lesson. Refer to this list as you study the dialogues.

MALE RELATIVES	FEMALE RELATIVES	EITHER OR BOTH SEXES
father	mother	parents
husband	wife	spouse
brother	sister	siblings
son	daughter	child (*plural:* children)
grandfather (grandpa)	grandmother (grandma)	grandparents
great-grandfather	great-grandmother	great-grandparents
uncle	aunt	cousin (child of either aunt or uncle)
son-in-law	daughter-in-law	
father-in-law	mother-in-law	in-laws
brother-in-law	sister-in-law	
grandson	granddaughter	grandchild (*plural:* grandchildren)
nephew	niece	
stepfather	stepmother	
half brother	half sister	
stepson	stepdaughter	stepchild (*plural:* stepchildren)
godson	goddaughter	godchild (*plural:* godchildren)
adopted son	adopted daughter	
foster son	foster daughter	foster child (*plural:* foster children)
foster father	foster mother	foster parents
		adolescent
		teenager
		youngster
		kid
		youth (young person)
		married
bachelor (unmarried man)	unmarried woman	single
fiancé	fiancée	
divorcé (*rarely used*)	divorcée	divorced
widower	widow	
		descendants
		ancestors
		orphan
		twins
		triplets
		quadruplets
		quintuplets

DIALOGUES

These dialogues make use of some of the terms contained in the Reference List of Family Relationships on the previous page. Refer to that list as you need it. The meanings of the boldface words and phrases should be clear to you from the way they are used in the dialogues. Answer the questions following each numbered dialogue.

1. **A:** Hi, Eddie. How's it going? Haven't seen you since our French final. How'd you make out?

    B: OK. What the . . . ? Am I seeing double? Maria, you didn't tell me you had a twin sister.

    A: You never asked me. This is Antonia. Toni, this is my friend, Eddie. He's the guy I was telling you about who was in my French class.

    C: Hi, Eddie. Nice to meet you. Maria tells me you speak French very well.

    B: Well, I try to. It's great meeting you, Toni. It's **incredible**! I can't **get over** it! You two are absolutely **identical**! You look exactly alike! Even your voices are the same! Do you always dress alike?

    A: No, not usually. But sometimes we do for fun. We like to see our friends **get us mixed up**.

    C: Sometimes even our parents can't **tell** us **apart at first glance**.

    A: When we were little, we had T-shirts that said "I'm Toni" and "I'm Maria." We used to exchange shirts to **play a trick on** Mom and Dad.

    B: I can see you two have great fun being twins. Well, sorry, I have to go. Hope to see you both again soon.

A and C: So long, Eddie.

Questions

1. When and where do you think this conversation might be taking place? Why do you think so?
2. What is **B**'s name?
3. Why does **B** think he is seeing double?
4. What is **C**'s real name? What is her nickname?
5. What does the expression **at first glance** mean?
6. Do you think that **A** is interested in **B**? Why do you think so?
7. What's another way of saying "play a trick on"?

2. **A:** How long have you and Jane known each other?

    B: Oh—for a long time. We **grew up** together. We lived in the same **neighborhood**. For a while, Jane was my **next-door neighbor**.

    C: (*Jane*) In fact, my **folks** used to **look after** Alan when his parents **went away**

for weekends. And when I was a teenager, I used to **baby-sit** for Alan's kid sister. Alan and his friends used to **come by** and **kid around** with me sometimes.

A: Maybe that's why you two **get along** so well together.

C: We didn't always. He used to **pick on** me a lot when we were little kids. You can't imagine the dumb things we used to **argue about**.

B: But your **folks** didn't let me **get away with** a thing, did they, Jane?

C: They sure didn't. They really **kept an eye on** both of us all the time.

A: Well, my congratulations to both of you. You make a very nice **couple**.

B: Thanks, Max.

C: We'll let you know when we set the date.

Questions

1. What's **A**'s name? **B**'s? **C**'s?
2. What's another way of saying "kid around"?
3. What's another way of saying "kid sister"?
4. What is still another meaning of the word **kid**?
5. What's another way of saying "he used to pick on me"?
6. How do you know that **C**'s parents watched the children carefully?
7. What word is used to refer to **C**'s parents in this dialogue?
8. How do you know that **B** and **C** are no longer teenagers?
9. What is the present relationship between **B** and **C**? How do you know?

3. **A:** You come from a large family, don't you? How many are there in your family? Your **immediate family**, I mean.

B: Well, I have three brothers and two sisters—and then there are my **maternal** grandparents. We're all very close.

A: You're very lucky. I was an **only child**. My mother **passed away** when I was two. After she **died** I was **brought up** by my **paternal** grandparents. They lived way out in the country. Sometimes I was pretty lonely. I always wished I had brothers and sisters to play with.

B: But your dad **remarried**, didn't he? Didn't he have any children by his second wife?

A: No, he didn't. You see, it took Dad a long time to **get over** my mother's **death**. He was a **widower** for years. In fact, he only remarried a couple of years ago—a **widow**. She had a son and a daughter, but they're both grown and married. I've never even met them. Dad is really my only **close relative**, and I hardly ever see him anymore. Sometimes I feel like an **orphan**.

B: I'm just the opposite. I have so many cousins and nieces and nephews that I can't **keep track of** them all.

A: Do you ever all **get together** at the same time? I mean all your cousins and aunts and uncles and so on? How big is your whole family, anyway?

B: You mean my whole family? All my relatives? Well, when we all get together for a **family reunion** every few years there are usually over two hundred of us. We have a whole community!

Questions

1. How many members are there in **B**'s immediate family?
2. What does the sentence "we're all very close" mean?
3. What's another way of saying "way out in the country"?
4. If **A**'s father had had children by his second wife, what relation would they be to **A**?
5. What relation to **A** are the children of her father's new wife?
6. Do you think that **A** and her father are close? Why or why not?
7. What's the difference in meaning between the word **couple** as it is used in this dialogue and the same word in Dialogue 2?
8. What's the difference between a **reunion** and a **meeting**?
9. What's the meaning of **get over** in this dialogue? Compare it with the meaning of the same word in Dialogue 1.

4. **A:** Are any of your grandparents still **alive**?

B: My mother's parents are both **dead**. My father's parents were **divorced** years ago. My grandmother lives with us. How about you?

A: All of them are still **living**. And all in good health, thank God. I even have a great-grandmother. Of course she's very **elderly**—ninety-two to be exact. She lives with my father's parents. My Grandma is seventy, and Grandpa is seventy-two.

B: Ninety-two! Is she getting **senile**, or does she still have all her **faculties**?

A: She's remarkable! A little **absent-minded now and then**, but who isn't? She **takes care of** the plants, and helps with the housework. She reads a lot, too. She says it helps her to stay young.

B: How about that! That's what all the studies say—that we women **outlive** men.

Questions

1. Which grandmother lives with **B**—maternal or paternal?
2. What's another word for **elderly**? (Look at the age of the great-grandmother.)
3. How old was the great-grandmother when **A**'s grandmother was born?
4. Is the great-grandmother still healthy? What makes you think so?
5. How do you know that the great-grandmother still has a sense of humor?
6. Are **A** and **B** men or women? (Look at **B**'s last remark.)
7. What does **outlive** mean?

5. **A:** Hi, Mary. Congratulations on the new grandchild! Was it a boy or a girl?

B: A girl. Twenty-one inches long, six and a half pounds. She's three weeks old already. Everybody says she **resembles** me.

A: I was going to ask you who* she **takes after**, but then I decided it's too soon to tell.

B: Right you are! As far as I'm concerned, babies **look like** what they are—babies!

A: Did they name her after anyone in the family?

B: She **was born** on my mother's birthday so they named her Amanda.

Questions

1. How do you know Mary is a grandmother?
2. Why does **A** use the word **new** to describe the baby?
3. To what do the measurements refer?
4. What do the words **resemble** and **take after** mean here?
5. To whom is **A** referring when she uses the word **they**?
6. What is the first name of the baby's great-grandmother?

VOCABULARY

All of these words and expressions have been used in the dialogues in this lesson. Study them carefully. They should become part of your vocabulary.

DIALOGUE 1

incredible
identical
at first glance
play a trick on
get (got) —— mixed up (S)
tell —— apart (S)
get over – unable to believe something

come (came) by – visit
go (went) away
get (got) along (with)
kid around
pick on – tease
get away with
keep (kept) an eye on
look after – take care of
argue about

DIALOGUE 2

neighborhood
next-door neighbor
folks
couple
baby-sit

DIALOGUE 3

immediate family
maternal
paternal
only child
family reunion

---

* In conversational English, *who* is normally used rather than *whom*.

close relative
widow, widower
die – pass away
death
orphan
remarry
keep track of
bring (brought) up (S) – raise
get over – recover from
get together

elderly
senile
faculties
divorce (v)
outlive (v)
absent-minded
now and then
take care of

DIALOGUE 5

resemble
take after
look like
be born

DIALOGUE 4

alive
dead
living (adj.)

QUESTIONS FOR CLASSROOM DISCUSSION

> **NOTE TO INSTRUCTOR:** Choose only those questions which are appropriate to the particular culture or situation in which you are teaching.

1. What is the age of your oldest living relative?

2. How many generations are represented in your family?

3. Where did you grow up—in the city or in the country?

4. Are there any relatives of yours that you've never met?

5. In your culture, is it a custom to hold family reunions? If so, about how often?

6. Were any of your ancestors famous or well-known?

7. With which member or members of your family do you get along best?

8. Who does most of the cooking in your home? Do you or other members of the family help with meal preparation?

9. Who does most of the housework? Which members of the family help with the housework? Do you clean your own room, for instance?

10. Do you think that husbands should share the housework with their wives?

11. In your culture, does the husband help in caring for the children?

12. In your culture, does the immediate family consist of the parents and their children, or does it include the grandparents?

13. In your culture, do parents ever employ teenagers to baby-sit for young children? If not, who takes care of the children when the parents go out for the evening?

14. All children disagree with their parents or siblings about something at one time or another. What sorts of things do members of your family argue about?

15. How does your family resolve disagreements or problems among various family members?

16. In your culture, how are older members of the family (aging grandparents, for instance) cared for? How do you feel about this?

17. If grandparents live with one of their children, what things determine with which child they live?

18. Do grandparents play any role in raising their grandchildren?

19. What are the advantages and/or disadvantages of being an only child?

20. When you were growing up, in what ways did you and your siblings pick on each other?

HOMEWORK

Part I. Vocabulary Building: A

Using the reference list at the beginning of this lesson and the dialogues as a guide, be prepared to answer these questions. Work them out with your friends if you wish.

Example: Your mother's parents are your maternal grandparents.

1. Your sister's or brother's son or daughter is your _____
   or _____ .

2. Your mother and father are your _____ .

3. Your brother or sister is your _____ .

4. Your father, mother, sisters, and brothers are your _____ .

5. Your brother's wife is your _____ .

6. Your sister's husband is your _____ .

7. Your aunt's or uncle's children are your _____ .

8. A child you baptized is your _____ .

9. A child whose mother and father are dead is an _____ .

10. Your mother's husband (not your father) is your _____ .

11. A person who has no sister or brother is an _____ _____ .

12. The son of your father's first wife is your _____ .

13. A man who has never married is a _____ or an
   _____ _____ . *(There are two possibilities.)*

14. A man whose wife has died is a _____ . →

15. The parents of your grandparents are your _____ .

Part II. Vocabulary Building: B

Use these words and expressions to complete the dialogues which follow. All of these vocabulary items have been used in the dialogues studied in this lesson.

immediate family	elderly	pick on
folks	playing tricks on	argue about
neighbors	first glance	go away
neighborhood	keep track of	tell apart (S)
alive	look alike (S)	takes after
dead	grow up	look after

1. **A:** Is your grandmother still _____ ?

   B: No. She's _____ . She died several years ago.

2. **A:** How many people are there in your _____ _____ ?

   B: There are six of us including my grandfather. He's _____ . He's ninety-two years old.

3. **A:** My kid sister and I used to get angry with each other and _____ _____ silly things.

   B: My brother and I did too. He used to _____ _____ me a lot. He was always _____ _____ _____ me.

4. **A:** Did you and Susan _____ _____ in the same _____ ?

   B: Yes, we did. In fact, we were next-door _____ for years.

5. **A:** Are your _____ going away for the weekend?

   B: Yes. My brother and I are going to _____ _____ the dog and cat.

6. **A:** Maria comes from a large family, doesn't she?

   B: She sure does. She says she has so many cousins she can't _____ _____ _____ all of them.

7. **A:** The twins _____ so much _____ , don't they?

   B: And how! At _____ _____ it's difficult to _____ them _____ .

8. **A:** Does your new grandchild look like your daughter or your son-in-law?

   B: Neither one. Everybody says she _____ _____ me. She has my nose and my mouth.

LISTENING COMPREHENSION EXERCISE: STUDENT'S ANSWER SHEET

1. ____ a) stayed.

   ____ b) visited.

   ____ c) bought.

2. ____ a) follows.

   ____ b) goes ahead of.

   ____ c) looks like.

3. ____ a) leave.

   ____ b) raise.

   ____ c) take.

4. ____ a) taking care of.

   ____ b) looking for.

   ____ c) calling for.

5. ____ a) recover from it.

   ____ b) believe it.

   ____ c) forget it.

6. ____ a) I confused one answer with the other.

   ____ b) I left out two questions.

   ____ c) I answered two questions correctly.

7. ____ a) friends.

   ____ b) grandparents.

   ____ c) parents.

8. ____ **a)** say something to them.

____ **b)** leave them alone.

____ **c)** distinguish one from the other.

9. ____ **a)** troublesome.

____ **b)** old.

____ **c)** sick.

10. ____ **a)** stay around.

____ **b)** make a date.

____ **c)** take a short trip.

CONVERSATION PRACTICE

> **NOTE TO INSTRUCTOR:** The following activity will use up a whole class session. Another way of doing it would be for each student to speak for a few minutes about his or her family, or bring a large-size family photograph and explain the relationship of everyone in the picture. Either way, you'll probably need a whole class period.

Following your instructor's directions, choose a classmate whom you do not know very well. Ask each other questions about your families. Be careful not to ask any embarrassing questions.

Here are some suggestions. Ask about:

1. Number of brothers and sisters.
2. Size of immediate family.
3. Profession or occupation of parents or other members of the family.
4. Where family members were born.
5. Any other interesting information.

Spend about five minutes gathering information and then arrange what you have learned in an interesting manner. Then, according to your instructor's directions, present the information you have learned about each other to the class. Keep your report short—not more than three minutes.

Let's Talk About Socializing

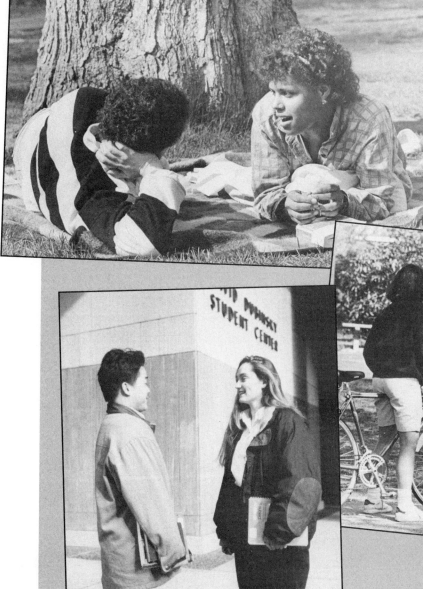

DIALOGUES

Study these dialogues and pay particular attention to the boldface expressions and two-word verbs. You may not have the occasion to use all of these vocabulary items, but you should be familiar with their usage so that you can understand them when you see them in print or when you hear another speaker using them.

1. **A:** Are you doing anything Saturday night?

    B: Well, I was sort of planning to work on a term paper. Why? What do you **have in mind**?

    A: Well, Toni's bringing her roommate home this weekend. Toni and I were wondering if you'd like to **double-date** with us. We'll probably **take in** a movie and go for a pizza or some ice cream afterwards.

    B: Gee. I don't know. I'm not much for **blind dates**. What's Toni's roommate like? Have you ever met her?

    A: No, but Toni says she's great. She's on the basketball team.

    B: Well, at least she and I would **have** something **in common** to **talk about**.

    A: So you'll go! Great! We'll **pick** you **up** about 8:00. OK?

    B: OK. I'll meet you downstairs in the lobby. I don't have to **dress up**, do I?

    A: Dress up to go to the movies? Are you kidding?

    B: OK. See you Saturday at 8:00.

Questions

1. What does the expression **double-date** mean?
2. How do you know **B** is a student?
3. Do you think that Toni is a college student who doesn't live at home? Why do you think so?
4. What is a "blind date"?
5. What does **B** mean when he says he's not much for blind dates?
6. How do you know that **B** likes basketball? Do you think that he may also play the game?
7. How do you know that **B** lives in an apartment house or in a dormitory?
8. What do you think the speakers in this dialogue will wear to go to the movies?

2. **A:** Hi, Laurie. It's Betty. (They are speaking by telephone.)

    B: Hi. How're you doing? Haven't seen you **in ages**.

    A: That's right. Not since last New Year's Eve, **as a matter of fact**.

    B: Heavens! Has it been that long? That was almost six months ago. It's terrible how we get so busy with our own work that we don't even have time to **socialize** with our old friends.

A: That's sort of why I'm calling. You know Sue's **getting married** next month. Some of the girls in the office are having a **shower** for her a week from Friday— that's the twenty-first—at my apartment. Can you come?

B: Gee, I'd love to. **Hold on** a minute while I check my **date book**. (After a minute or two.) I can make it. I don't **have** anything **on** for that night. What time?

A: About 7:30. Everybody's bringing a dish. Could you bring one of your special casseroles?

B: Sure. How many people are you planning to have?

A: We're not sure yet. We're trying to **get in touch** with some of the gang who went to college with us. Bring something that will serve eight or ten.

B: OK. I'll **whip up** something nice. What are you planning to do about a gift or gifts?

A: That's something we haven't **decided on** yet. We're probably going to ask everybody to **chip in** for one gift. I'll **let** you **know** later on this week. Glad you can come. Bye now.

B: Bye. See you on the twenty-first.

Questions

1. In what month does this conversation take place? How do you know?
2. What's another way of saying "in ages"?
3. How do you know that Laurie, Betty, and Sue all went to the same college?
4. What is another way of saying "get in touch with"? How might you get in touch with a person you haven't seen in a long time?
5. How do you know that Betty and Sue work in the same office?
6. What does Laurie mean when she says she doesn't "have anything on" for the twenty-first?
7. What is the meaning of **shower** in this dialogue? Can you think of two other very common meanings of this word?
8. What's the meaning of the word **gang** in this dialogue?
9. What does Laurie mean when she says she'll "whip up" a casserole? What is a casserole?
10. What's another way of saying "I'll let you know"?

3. **A:** You and Mario make a nice couple. How long have you been **going together**?

B: You mean **going out together** or **going together**?

A: I mean how long have you been **going steady**? When did you start **getting serious**?

B: Only about two months ago. Before that we were both **dating** other people **once in a while**. Then we both realized that we preferred each other's company to anybody else's. So-o-o we decided we wanted to go steady. What about you and Michael?

A: Oh, we're just good friends. We have a lot of things in common. Both of us like to listen to jazz and we like the same kind of movies and sports. But mostly we just like to sit and talk about all kinds of things. But there's nothing between us.

B: Hm-m-m-m. Doesn't sound like that to me.

Questions

1. What's the difference between **going out with** somebody and **going with** somebody? (You can probably guess the difference from the way the expressions are used in this dialogue.)

2. What does "we were both dating other people" mean?

3. What does the expression **going steady** imply?

4. What's another expression that means the same as **once in a while**?

5. What does **A** mean when she says "there's nothing between us"?

6. Does **B** believe what **A** says about her relationship with Michael? How can you tell?

4. A: Your sister is very cute. I'd like to **ask** her **for a date**. Do you know if she has a steady boyfriend?

B: Not at the moment. She **went with** a guy for a while, but they **broke up**. As far as I know she's not dating anyone in particular right now.

A: Do you think she'd **go out with** me?

B: How should I know? Why don't you **call** her **up** and ask her?

A: I'm afraid she might **turn** me **down**. I was hoping you'd **put in a good word for** me.

B: Oh, come on, man! I have more important things to do than to **get involved in** my kid sister's social life. Call her up, for Pete's sake. Our number's in the book. Under my mother's name. M. C. Martin.

Questions

1. What does the expression **ask for a date** mean?

2. Why do you think **A** is afraid **B**'s sister will turn him down?

3. What's another way of saying "put in a good word for"?

4. How do you know that **B**'s sister is younger than he is?

5. What does **B** mean by "the book"? Why do you think he didn't just give **A** the number instead of telling him to look it up?

6. Why do you think the telephone number is listed under **B**'s mother's name instead of under his father's name?

5. A: Hi, there. Looks like you could use some help. Let me **give** you **a hand**. Where are you going with all that stuff, anyway?

B: Thanks, Ricki. Just across the street to the Student Center. My class is having its Spring Dance next Saturday. Two other girls and I are in charge of decorations.

A: (They walk toward the Student Center.) Do you **have a date** for the dance yet? How about asking me?

B: What a coincidence! You won't believe this, but I was going to call you up tonight and ask you to **go with** me. Sure, I'd love to go with you. Just set the box down in the corner. Thanks a lot.

A: Then it's a **date**. What time shall I pick you up?

B: Oh—about 8:15, I guess.

A: Well—I have to run. I have to study for a final exam tomorrow morning. See you Saturday.

B: So long, Ricki. Thanks again for helping me.

A: Don't mention it. So long.

Questions

1. How do you know that **B** is a girl?

2. What do you think **B** might be carrying in the box? In other words, what sorts of things would you use as decorations for a party?

3. In what month do you think the conversation takes place? Mention two clues that the dialogue contains.

4. What is the coincidence that **B** mentions?

5. What's the difference in meaning of the verb **go with** in this dialogue and in Dialogue 4 (past tense)?

6. Why is **A** in a hurry? What time of day do you think the conversation takes place?

6. **A:** Hi, Janet. How are you?

B: Carmen? Hi. It's good to hear from you. What's up?

A: Well, we've finally finished remodeling our house and we are **having** some friends **over** for an **open house** to celebrate. It's next Saturday. Nothing fancy—just drinks and snacks.

B: Congratulations! I heard you were making some renovations. What kind of improvements did you make?

A: Well, we **put in** a new kitchen and **did over** the living room. Then we had the whole house painted. Come over and see for yourself.

B: Saturday? Oh, I just remembered. Peggy's seventh-grade class is having a party at the junior high school. I promised to be one of the **chaperones**.

A: Gee, that's too bad. Sorry you can't make it. Why don't you give me a call some afternoon and **stop by** for a few minutes. I'd really like you to see the house.

B: OK. I'll do that. Thanks for calling anyway.

Questions

1. How is this conversation taking place? How can you tell?

2. How do you know that **A** and **B** have not seen or spoken to each other recently? Do you think they're good friends? Why or why not?

3. What do you think **A** means by "an open house"?

4. How do you know that **A** and **B** do not live close to each other?

5. Who is Peggy?

6. Is there a difference in meaning between the expressions **have over** and **come over**? Explain the meaning of each.

7. What does the expression **do over** mean as it is used in this dialogue?

8. Why can't **B** accept the invitation?

9. Can you explain what the role of a chaperone is?

10. What's another way of saying "give me a call"?

VOCABULARY

The following words and expressions have been used in the dialogues of this lesson. Reread the dialogues and study the vocabulary items listed for each dialogue.

DIALOGUE 1

blind date
double date (v)
have in mind *or* have (something)
   in mind (S)
have ——— in common (S)
take (took) in – attend
talk about (S)
dress up
pick up – come to get (S)

DIALOGUE 2

shower – party
date book
socialize
in ages
as a matter of fact – in fact
get married
hold on – wait a minute
get in touch with
whip up (S) – prepare quickly
decide on
chip in (for) – contribute money

let know (S)
have on (S)

DIALOGUE 3

once in a while – now and then
go together – have a romantic attachment
go out together
go steady
get serious (adj.) – have an important
   relationship
date (v) – to have social engagements
   with

DIALOGUE 4

ask for a date
put in a good word for
get involved in – be concerned with
go with – have a romantic attachment
go out with – have a date
break (broke) up
call up (S)
turn down (S) – reject, refuse an invitation

DIALOGUE 5

date (n)
have a date
give (someone) a hand (S)
go with – accompany

DIALOGUE 6

open house
chaperone
have over (S) – invite
put in – install
do over (S) – redecorate
stop by

QUESTIONS FOR CLASS DISCUSSION

> **NOTE TO INSTRUCTOR:** Use only those questions which would be appropriate for the culture or situation in which you are teaching or for the amount of class time you plan to allow for the activity.

1. How do young men and women in your culture get to know each other?

2. In your culture, are young people chaperoned? That is, are young people accompanied by an older person when they go to a party or some other social function? Who might that older person or persons be? How do young people feel about this custom?

3. Do you or did you and your friends go out in groups or as couples?

4. About how old were you when you started to date; that is, go out alone with someone of the opposite sex?

5. How frequently did you or do you double-date?

6. How do you feel about accepting a blind date?

7. How do you feel about the practice of going steady? How old should a young man or woman be before he or she starts to go steady?

8. In your culture, is it acceptable for a young woman to date several different young men before choosing a steady partner?

9. In your culture, is it acceptable for girls to ask boys to go out with them? What do you think of this practice?

10. Are the dating customs of young people who go away to school different from those students who live at home while attending a college or a university?

11. Is it a custom to hold "an open house" in your culture? On what kind of occasions?

12. Is it a custom to extend informal invitations to social functions over the telephone?

13. If you were planning a dinner party, how long ahead of time would you invite your guests? A week? Two weeks?

14. If you are planning to serve a meal at 7:30 PM, at what time do you ask your guests to arrive?

15. If you have an invitation for dinner at 7:30 PM, at what time do you usually arrive?

16. If a friend invites you to a party which is to begin at 8:00 PM, at what time will you probably arrive?

17. In your culture, if you have to turn down an invitation, what do you say or do?

18. In your culture, when you are invited to someone's house for dinner, is it a custom to take a gift? Would you take a box of candy, a bottle of wine, or some flowers perhaps?

19. In your culture, is it a custom for friends to chip in to buy a special present for a person?

20. In your culture, is it a custom for a girl's friends to have a party for her when she is about to be married? Would a man's friends give a party for him if he is about to be married?

HOMEWORK

Part I. Using Two-Word Verbs

These dialogues contain words and expressions similar in meaning to some of the two-word verbs listed below. In the space provided, write the two-word verb which is closest in meaning to the boldface portion of the statement. Use the past tense form of the verb whenever necessary.

chip in	take in	go with
have over (S)	turn down (S)	do over
stop by	whip up (S)	call up (S)
put in (S)	go out with	talk about

Example: **A:** Who does Maria **have a date with** this Saturday?
B: She told me she's **going out with** Lionel.

1. A: Has Bob **phoned** you yet about our plans for the weekend?

   B: Yes, he _____ me _____ last night.

2. A: What sort of dish can you **prepare quickly** for our class party?

   B: I'll _____ _____ a very simple dessert of some kind.

3. A: When are they going to **install** the new telephone system in your office?

   B: They're supposed to _____ it _____ next month.

4. A: Why don't you **visit** me some afternoon this week?

   B: I'll _____ _____ on my way home from shopping on Saturday.

5. A: Did you **invite** any friends to help you celebrate your anniversary?

   B: Yes, we _____ some people _____ last Sunday.

6. A: Tom said he was very sorry that he had to **reject** your offer.

   B: I was afraid that he'd _____ it _____ .
   He's very busy right now.

7. A: Did you **attend** the ceremony last night?

   B: No. We _____ _____ a movie instead.

8. A: Did you **redecorate** your whole apartment?

   B: No, we just _____ _____ the living room and the kitchen.

9. A: We've decided that we're all going to **share the cost** of the present for Sally.

   B: Fine. Just let me know how much you'd like me to _____ _____ for it.

10. A: My grandmother needs someone to **accompany** her to the wedding. She doesn't want to go alone.

   B: Please tell her I'll be glad to _____ _____ her. I'll pick her up in my car.

Part II. Vocabulary Building

Use these expressions and two-word verbs in sentences or dialogues of your own. Be sure that the meaning of each one is clear in the sentence or dialogue that you write.

date book	put in a good word for	dress up
blind date	get involved in	go steady
have in mind *or*	get married	break up
have —— in mind	once in a while	let know (S)
(choose one)	have on (S)	decide on
get in touch with	go together, go with	double-date (v)
have —— in common	*(choose one)*	

> **NOTE:** Of course, you may also use other vocabulary items from this lesson or from previous lessons.

LISTENING COMPREHENSION EXERCISE: STUDENT'S ANSWER SHEET

Part I

1. ____ **a)** We're going to see a movie in a theater.

____ **b)** We're going to watch a TV movie.

____ **c)** We're going to use a movie camera.

2. ____ **a)** I'm not wearing any clothes.

____ **b)** I don't have any other plans.

____ **c)** I don't have anything more important to do.

3. ____ **a)** Chris will buy some food on the way home from work.

____ **b)** Chris will prepare something quickly.

____ **c)** Chris will ask a friend to bring something for dinner.

4. ____ **a)** I'll get in touch with you.

____ **b)** I'll call you up.

____ **c)** I'll come to get you.

5. ____ **a)** visit some friends.

____ **b)** invite some friends to our house.

____ **c)** go out with some friends.

Part II

1. ____ **a)** two pieces of fruit.

____ **b)** two calendar days.

____ **c)** a social engagement with another couple.

2. ____ **a)** Please shake hands with me.

____ **b)** Please help me.

____ **c)** Please let me take your hand.

3. ____ **a)** We like very ordinary things.

____ **b)** We are interested in the same things.

____ **c)** We both have the same things.

4. ____ **a)** a building with many windows.

____ **b)** a house with a big open terrace.

____ **c)** a kind of party.

5. ____ **a)** What are you planning?

____ **b)** What are you cooking?

____ **c)** What are you imagining?

CONVERSATION PRACTICE

Together with one or two of your classmates, work out a conversation about one of the following situations. There should be at least three exchanges; that is, **A B, A B, A B,** or **A B C, A B C, A B C**. After you have practiced your conversation, present it to the class according to your instructor's directions. Use expressions and verbs which appear in the dialogues of this lesson.

1. You and a group of friends are planning a surprise party for another friend who is about to get married. You and another friend or two are discussing where and when the party should be held, and what the group should do about presenting the girl with a gift or gifts.

2. **A** sees **B** carrying several large packages and offers to help her or him. **B** accepts **A's** offer and they have a conversation during which one (either **A** or **B**) mentions a party that is coming up and invites the other one to go. The invitation is accepted and the friends arrange to meet at an appropriate time.

3. **A** invites **B** to go to a picnic, but **B** already has an appointment for that day and has to turn down the invitation. However, **B** suggests that they — **A** and **B** — could plan another outing on a later date and **A** agrees.

4. You and your husband (or wife or girlfriend or boyfriend) are planning a party to celebrate an occasion. (You decide what the occasion is.) You are calling friends and decide to call a particular friend. That friend turns down the invitation saying that he or she already has an engagement that day or night. End the conversation in an appropriate manner.

5. With one or two classmates, make up a conversation using some of the following expressions: ask for a date, go out with, go out together, go steady, go with.

6. A's girlfriend (or boyfriend) has a visiting friend. A asks B if he or she would like to do something (you decide what the social occasion is) with A, the girlfriend or boyfriend, and the visitor. B accepts after a brief discussion and they arrange to meet.

7. With one or more classmates, make up a conversation based on a situation similar to one in a dialogue in this lesson.

Review Lesson I

USING TWO-WORD VERBS

Part I. Class Exercise

Here are several two-word verbs you have studied in Lessons 1 through 6. Some of them are appropriate to use in the dialogues which follow. Write the verb which you think belongs in the blank space in each of the dialogues. You will have to use the past tense -ed ending of some of the verbs. After you have completed the dialogues, read them aloud with a classmate. In a few cases, more than one verb may be correct for a particular dialogue.

turn down (S)   look like   hand in (S)
drop off (S)   hand back (S)   fill out (S)
make out   pick up (S)   take out (S)
turn off (S)   tell apart (S)   copy over (S)
worry about   call up (S)

1. **A:** Have you heard from Ana lately?

   B: Yes, as a matter of fact, she _____ me _____ last night.
   We talked for almost an hour.

2. **A:** I'm sorry. I wrote the homework assignment in pencil instead of in ink. Can I
   _____ it _____ ?

   B: Don't _____ _____ it this time. Hand
   your assignment in the way it is. But next time, remember to follow instructions.

3. **A:** Where are you going?

   B: To the drugstore. I have to _____ _____ some
   toothpaste.

4. **A:** I haven't finished my assignment yet, professor.

   B: That's OK. But please _____ it _____ tomorrow.

5. **A:** Did you hear the announcement?

   B: Not very well. I couldn't _____ _____
   everything he said.

6. **A:** Are you going home now?

   B: Yes, but first I have to _____ _____ a book at the library. It's due today.

7. **A:** Is the radio still on in the living room?

   B: No. I _____ it _____ when the news broadcast ended.

8. **A:** What did you do on the first day of class?

   B: We _____ _____ some information on a card.

9. **A:** I wasn't in class today. Did Professor Watkins return the homework assignment?

   B: Yes, she _____ it _____ with her corrections.

10. **A:** Did you go to Nancy's open house last Saturday?

   B: No, I had to _____ _____ her invitation because I had another engagement.

Part II. Homework Exercise

Many two-word verbs have more than one meaning. All of the verbs listed below have been used in Lessons 1 through 6 and all of them have been used with two different meanings. Write sentences or dialogues of your own using each of these items. The meanings of some of the verbs are given in parentheses after the verb. Use some of the verbs in the past tense.

go with (accompany) *Lesson 6*
go with (have a romantic attachment) *Lesson 6*
go off (stop functioning, as with electricity, air conditioning) *Lesson 3*
go off (ring, sound) *Lesson 3*
make out (understand) *Lesson 2*
make out (succeed) *Lesson 4*
pick up (go and get someone) *Lesson 6*
pick up (buy, obtain) *Lesson 1*
do over (do again) *Lesson 2*
do over (redecorate) *Lesson 6*
take out (borrow, as with books from a library) *Lesson 4*
take out (remove; to make available for use) *Lesson 2*

VOCABULARY BUILDING

Part I. Lessons 1 – 3

Here are several vocabulary items you have studied in Lessons 1 through 3. Complete
the following dialogues by writing the correct words or expressions in the blanks.
Be sure to use the correct tense and form of the verbs. After you have completed the
dialogues, practice reading them aloud with a classmate.

nickname	lose	make a date
maiden name	fast	looking forward to
given name	slow	(be) absent from
hometown	gain	run into
oversleep	set the alarm	

1. **A:** Paul was _____ our seven o'clock class today.

    Do you know why he didn't come?

    B: Yeah. He _____ . He forgot to _____

    _____ _____ and he didn't wake up until eight o'clock.

2. **A:** Do you have the time? My watch says it's four o'clock but I don't think it's that late.

    My watch has been running _____ . It _____

    about twenty minutes a day.

    B: Mine is just the opposite. It runs _____ . It _____

    about fifteen minutes a day. Sometimes I'm late for appointments.

3. **A:** Jane and I are from the same _____ . But I hadn't seen

    her for a long time until I _____ _____ her yesterday.
    Since the three of us are going to be officemates she wants to meet you.

    B: I'm _____ _____ _____

    meeting her. Let's _____ _____ _____ for lunch

    next Saturday.

4. **A:** My friend's name is Peter, Peter Allen. But everybody calls him Pete. That's

    his _____ .

    B: What a coincidence. My mother's _____ _____

    was Allen before she married my father.

Part II. Lessons 4 – 6

Here are several vocabulary items you have studied in Lessons 4 through 6. Complete the following dialogues by writing the correct words or expressions in the blanks. *Be sure to use the correct tense and form of the verbs.* After you have completed the dialogues, practice reading them aloud with a classmate.

couple	maternal	pass (a course)
only child	paternal	have —— in common (S)
siblings	drop (a course)	keep an eye on
folks	fail (a course)	double-date
close relatives	take (a course)	have in mind

1. **A:** Do you and Tom often _____ with Helen and Fred?

 B: Yes, we do. They're a very nice _____ . They like to do

 the same things we do. We _____ a lot of things _____

 _____ .

2. **A:** I was taking sixteen credits but I _____ a course because

 it was very difficult. I _____ all my other courses, though.

 B: I got an *F* on the biology final exam, so I _____ the course.

 Now I'll have to _____ the course again in summer school.

3. **A:** Will you please watch the children while I run next door for a minute?

 B: Certainly. I'll be glad to _____ _____ _____

 _____ them.

4. **A:** Is this correct? My mother's parents are my _____

 grandparents.

 B: That's right, and your father's parents are your _____

 grandparents.

5. **A:** My _____ wanted to have a large family so there are five

 of us children.

 B: You're lucky. I don't have any _____ . I'm an _____

 _____ . My parents are my only _____

 _____ .

REVIEW LESSON I — LISTENING COMPREHENSION
EXERCISE: STUDENT'S ANSWER SHEET

1. ____ **a)** repeated.

____ **b)** discussed.

____ **c)** solved.

2. ____ **a)** write.

____ **b)** investigate.

____ **c)** find.

3. ____ **a)** write on the other side of the paper.

____ **b)** write it again in its present form.

____ **c)** revise it completely.

4. ____ **a)** make a suggestion.

____ **b)** bring a friend.

____ **c)** contribute some money.

5. ____ **a)** I didn't pay attention.

____ **b)** I fell asleep.

____ **c)** I left the room.

6. ____ **a)** put a mark next to the words.

____ **b)** erase the words.

____ **c)** draw a line through the words.

7. ____ **a)** draw a line through the verbs.

____ **b)** put accent marks on the verbs.

____ **c)** draw a line beneath the verbs.

8. _____ **a)** money to pay for my courses.

_____ **b)** money to pay for my food.

_____ **c)** money to pay the rent.

9. _____ **a)** sleepy.

_____ **b)** sick.

_____ **c)** bored.

10. _____ **a)** I'll sleep for a short time.

_____ **b)** I'll have a snack.

_____ **c)** I'll go for a walk.

11. _____ **a)** I've heard of it.

_____ **b)** I understand it.

_____ **c)** I'll figure it out later.

12. _____ **a)** a close relative.

_____ **b)** a former student.

_____ **c)** another professor.

13. _____ **a)** He resembles a member of my family.

_____ **b)** I think I've seen him before.

_____ **c)** I think he's a distant relative.

14. _____ **a)** I turned on the alarm at six.

_____ **b)** I turned off the alarm at six.

_____ **c)** I wanted the alarm to ring at six.

15. _____ **a)** schedule.

_____ **b)** responsibilities.

_____ **c)** problems.

8

Let's Talk About Food

FRUITS

apple

pear

peaches

grapes

cherries

watermelon

orange

grapefruit

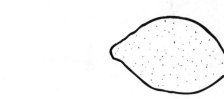
lemon

pineapple

banana

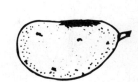
mango

plums

papaya

strawberries

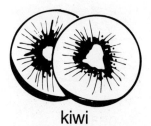
kiwi

apricot

cantaloupe

VEGETABLES

tomato

lettuce

broccoli

cabbage

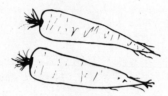

carrots

celery

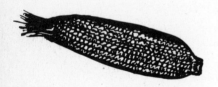

beans

pumpkin

potatoes

corn

plantains

okra

onion

garlic

eggplant

asparagus

cucumber

peas

DIALOGUES

In studying these dialogues, pay special attention to the boldface vocabulary items. Some of the words and expressions you will recognize. You should be able to learn the meanings of the others from the way in which they are used in the dialogues. If you are not familiar with the various items of food mentioned, your instructor will probably explain them to you. If not, you can find most of them defined in a good English-English dictionary.

1. **A:** I'm so tired from **copying down** all these notes. I think I'll **take a break**. I only have a few more pages to go.

B: It's almost noon. You've **been at** it for over an hour. If you're hungry there are a few **leftovers** from last night in the refrigerator—some **veal stew**, a little bit of rice, or I could make you a **tuna-fish** sandwich. Would you **care for** something?

A: No, thanks. I can usually **do without** lunch. Besides, I got up late and had a big breakfast. I could use a cold drink—a diet soda or something.

B: Sure. I'll get you something right away. If you don't mind, I'll have some of that veal while you take a break. I have no trouble with my **appetite**.

A: Go right ahead. It's really not a good idea to **skip** a meal, but I'm not hungry now. I'll probably have a **snack** when I get home.

B: I try not to eat anything between **meals** myself—helps me **keep** my weight **down**.

Questions

1. Where do you think this dialogue may be taking place? Are the speakers men or women? Why do you think so?

2. About what time was it when **A** started copying down the notes? How do you know?

3. What's another way of saying "you've been at it"?

4. What sort of notes do you think **A** might be copying? Why do you think **A** might be doing this?

5. What are leftovers?

6. What is a stew? What are some of the ingredients it might contain?

7. What does **A** mean by "I can usually do without lunch"?

8. What is a snack? What kind of food would you eat for a snack? Would the choice of food depend on the time of day?

9. What does **B** mean when he or she says that not eating between meals helps keep his or her weight down?

2. **A:** Hi, Lucy. Are you **going out** to lunch?

   B: Heavens! Is it **lunch time** already? **Actually**, I hadn't thought about it until you mentioned it. I had a snack during my **coffee break** and I'm **not** hungry **at all**.

   A: Well, when you do get hungry, **drop by** my office. I brought some **homemade lasagna** that was **left over** from last night's dinner. There's more than enough for one person. My husband made it. It's one of his **specialties**.

   B: Thanks, Chris. Right now, I don't feel like having anything **heavy** for lunch. That snack really **filled** me **up**. How're you going to **warm up** the lasagna anyway?

   A: In the **microwave**, of course; since they put that in, nobody in my office goes out to eat anymore.

   B: Well, if I decide not to go out, I'll call you and let you know. But, please, don't wait for me.

Questions

1. Where does this dialogue take place?

2. How do you know that Lucy and Chris don't work in the same office?

3. Are the women speaking to each other in person or on the telephone? Why do you think so?

4. What's another way of saying **drop by**? (In Lesson 5, Dialogue 2, you'll find a synonym for this verb.)

5. Would a person necessarily have to drink coffee during a coffee break?

6. What's another way of saying "I'm not hungry at all"?

7. What is lasagna and what ingredients would it contain? In what country did it originate?

8. How do you know that Chris's husband is a good cook?

9. Can you think of other foods that could be called "heavy"?

10. What is the microwave that **A** refers to? Who do you think the word **they** refers to in that sentence?

11. What's another way of saying **warm up** in this dialogue?

12. What does the word **actually** mean?

3. **A:** Do you have any plans for Sunday morning?

   B: Well, Don and I are planning to **drive out** to the beach around noon, depending on the weather.

   A: How about joining us for **brunch**? I was going to **stir up** some special **waffles**, but Wally wants to **try out** a new **recipe** for **quiche**.

   B: You know, we're not really breakfast people, but I guess brunch would be OK. Let me check with Don first and then I'll let you know. What time were you planning on eating?

   A: Around eleven. You could drive out to the beach after that.

   B: I'll **give you a buzz** tonight. Thanks for the invitation.

Questions

1. Why do you think **B** says they're going to **drive out** to the beach? Where do you think they may live?

2. Why does **B** say "depending on the weather"? How would the weather affect going to the beach?

3. How else could you ask, "How about joining us?"

4. Do you know what a brunch is? How do you think the word originated?

5. Do you know the difference between **waffles** and **pancakes**? Can you explain to the class?

6. What does **B** mean by "we're not really breakfast people"?

7. What is a quiche? What are some of the usual ingredients?

At the Snack Bar

4. **A:** Let's get something **light**. It's been a **hectic** day and I don't **feel like** eating a lot.

B: I just want some black coffee, myself.

A: On an **empty stomach**? You drink black coffee on an empty stomach?

B: Well, maybe you're right. Maybe I should eat something first. I'll have an egg salad sandwich. I used to love egg salad sandwiches, but I haven't had eggs in ages.

A: How come?

B: Well, when I went to see my doctor around the first of the year, my **cholesterol count** was way up. So I had to **quit** eating red meat and cheese and whole milk and eggs. I used to have two eggs every morning—fried, sunny side up, scrambled, soft boiled—with bacon or ham.

A: No wonder your cholesterol count was too high. Have you **brought** it **down** yet?

B: Yeah. It's taken me three months, but my cholesterol level is down. So I guess I can have an egg salad sandwich.

A: I think I'll have a **grilled** cheese sandwich and a soda. I think my cholesterol level is OK.

B: Don't be so sure. That's what I thought, and boy, was I wrong!

Questions

1. What kind of day would you consider to be a hectic day?

2. What are some examples of **light** food?

3. Why do you think **A** is so concerned about **B** drinking black coffee on an empty stomach?

4. What would an egg salad sandwich consist of? Can you mention other kinds of salad sandwiches?

5. What do you know about cholesterol? What does **B** mean by "my cholesterol count was way up"? What can happen when a person's cholesterol count is too high?

6. Discuss with your instructor the various ways of preparing eggs mentioned in this dialogue. Can you mention any other ways of serving eggs?

7. During which month does this dialogue take place?

8. What's the difference between a cheese sandwich and a grilled cheese sandwich?

5. **A:** Syd wants you and me to **be in charge of refreshments** for the party on Saturday. What sort of food do you think we should take?

B: I'd say **ready-made** food. You know—**cold cuts**, cheese, sandwich bread, **potato chips**. Maybe some lettuce and tomatoes and some fruit—and **soda**.

A: Syd said the guys would **take care of** the soda and the beer. I could **bake** some chocolate chip **cookies**. People might like something sweet.

B: I didn't know you did your own **baking**. I never bake, myself—too much trouble.

A: I've been baking ever since I was a kid, especially cookies. This recipe is no big deal. I can **mix up** a **batch in a jiffy**.

B: Well, I'm a **fast food** fan, myself: **pizza**, **hamburgers**, **hot dogs**, **fried chicken**, **tacos**, a roast beef sandwich . . . you name it.

A: I call that **junk food**, not fast food.

B: It may be junk food, but I love it. Besides, I hate to cook.

A: Well, let's go to the **supermarket** before it closes. We don't have much time left today. Tomorrow is my **day off**, but it's all **taken up**.

B: So is mine. Let's go.

Questions

1. What are **refreshments**?

2. What is **ready-made** food? Can you think of any other examples of this kind of food?

3. For what other things could you use the verb **mix up** besides a batch of cookies?

4. What does **A** mean by "this recipe is no big deal"?

5. What is fast food?

6. Why do you think **A** refers to fast food as junk food?

7. What is another way of saying "my day is all taken up"?

8. What is the difference between baking something and boiling it?

9. What does the expression **in a jiffy** mean?

10. What is another way of saying "my day off"?

6. **A:** I'm going over to the **grocery store**. What kind of meat should I get for the week?

B: Well, you said you wanted to eat less **red meat**. So let's plan on having chicken, **veal**, fish, and **turkey**. This way we'd eat red meat only about twice a week.

A: We could also have a vegetable dish as our **main course** one night.

B: Why not? I could make some **pasta** with vegetables.

A: Don't make it **hot** and **spicy** like that Mexican dish you prepared the other day. It's delicious, but my stomach can't handle it.

B: Don't worry. I'll just use regular Italian **seasoning**. It gives it a special **flavor**.

A: That sounds better. Anyway, what should I get?

B: Get some chicken **breasts**, veal **chops**, fresh fish, turkey **thighs**, and a couple of T-bone **steaks**. Oh, also get some **lean ground beef** for hamburgers.

A: OK. I should be back in about an hour.

B: Maybe you could stop at the **farmers' market** and get some vegetables, both green and yellow. Whatever you prefer. Oh, and there's a sale on **shrimp** at the corner **deli** near the market . . .

A: Hold it, hold it. I don't have much time, so it'll be the grocery store today. Tomorrow I'll get the rest of the things. I'd better go before you add more stuff to the list.

B: Sorry. I just thought you could do all the shopping today instead of **making** another **trip** tomorrow.

Questions

1. In what way does a grocery store differ from a supermarket?

2. Why do you think **A** says, "I'm going over to the grocery store," instead of just, "I'm going"?

3. Which meats are considered red meat? To what category of food do chicken and turkey belong?

4. Why do you think **A** wants to eat less red meat?

5. What is pasta? Can you mention some examples of it?

6. What does **hot** mean in this dialogue? What is the difference between hot food and spicy food?

7. What does **A** mean by "my stomach can't handle it"?

8. What is lean meat?

9. What is **seasoning** as it is used in this dialogue?

10. What other kinds of chops can you get besides veal chops?

11. What is a farmers' market? What do you think you can buy there?

12. Can you think of some examples of green vegetables? Yellow vegetables?

13. What is the word **deli** a short form of? What do you think you can buy in that kind of store?

14. What is the difference in meaning between **taking a trip** and **making a trip**?

7. A: Hello.

B: Hi, Jack. Sorry to **bother** you. But I need a **favor** from you. I need an easy-to-fix recipe for dinner tonight, and you're the only person I can **count on**.

A: Sure.

B: Sarah just called me. She's invited some friends over for dinner. I'm loaded with work so I can't go home early. I just don't know what to make. Do you have any ideas for me?

A: OK, Jed. How many people do you expect?

B: Two, but it'll be four—counting Sarah and me.

A: Now, let me think for a moment.

B: I just want to cook something simple like roast beef or baked chicken . . . nothing **fancy**.

A: How about serving some London **broil** like the one you had here the other day?

B: Oh, that was delicious! Does it take a lot of time to prepare?

A: No, it's very easy. Why don't you stop at the supermarket on your way home? Get a piece of London broil and a can of onion soup. **Pour** the **soup** over the meat and add about half a cup of red wine. Put the meat in the **oven** at 350 degrees for about an hour. And that's it.

B: That's perfect! I can serve it with rice and **zucchini** and salad. For **dessert** Sarah can pick up something at the **pastry** shop. Problem solved! Thanks, Jack. You're a special friend and a wonderful **chef**. I knew I could **depend on** you for advice.

A: Any time. Enjoy your dinner.

B: Thanks a million.

Questions

1. Who's going to do the cooking — **A** or Sarah?
2. What does **B** mean when he asks Jack for an easy-to-fix recipe?
3. What does **B** mean when he says he is loaded with work?
4. When **A** says, "Why don't you stop at the supermarket?", is he asking **B** a question or making a suggestion? What is another way of expressing the same idea?
5. What other verb in this dialogue means the same as **count on**?
6. What sort of food do you think is sold at a pastry shop? (See **B**'s last statement.)

VOCABULARY

The following lists of words and expressions have all been used in the dialogues of this lesson. In reviewing these vocabulary items, refer to the dialogues.

DIALOGUE 1

leftovers
veal
stew
appetite

snack
meal
tuna fish
take a break
copy down (S)
be at (something) – do

care for – like, have a taste for
do without
keep down (S) – control
skip (a meal)

DIALOGUE 2

lunch time
specialty
coffee break
microwave (oven)
lasagna
actually
homemade
heavy
not (busy, hungry, sleepy, etc.) at all
left over
go out
drop by
warm up (S) – heat

DIALOGUE 3

brunch
waffles
recipe
quiche
give (someone) a buzz
drive out
stir up (S)
try out (S)

DIALOGUE 4

cholesterol count, level
stomach
light (adj.)
hectic
empty
grilled (adj.)
quit
bring down (S) – lower, make less
feel like

DIALOGUE 5

refreshments
cold cuts
potato chips
soda
cookie
pizza
hamburger
hot dog
taco
chicken
supermarket
fast food
junk food
batch (of cookies, waffles, etc.)
day off
ready-made
fried (adj.)
bake (v), baking (n)
in a jiffy
be in charge of
take care of – provide
mix up (S)
take up – fill, occupy

DIALOGUE 6

grocery store
farmers' market
main course
seasoning
flavor
red meat
pasta
veal
turkey
chops
steak
shrimp
ground beef
breast
thigh
deli – delicatessen
spicy
hot
lean (adj.)
make a trip

DIALOGUE 7

broil
zucchini
dessert
pastry
favor

oven
chef
loaded (with)
fancy
bother (v)
count on – depend on
pour over (S)

QUESTIONS FOR CLASS DISCUSSION

NOTE TO INSTRUCTOR: Choose only those questions appropriate to your
particular classroom situation and to the amount of class time you
plan to allow for this activity.

---

1. What is your idea of a good breakfast? Do you usually eat one?

2. For you, what does a typical lunch consist of?

3. Do you ever eat brunch? If so, what sort of food do you eat?

4. What are some of your favorite fruits?

5. What are some of your favorite yellow vegetables? Green vegetables? Are there any vegetables you don't care for? Why do nutritionists stress the importance of including vegetables in your diet?

6. How do you prefer to have your eggs prepared?

7. What do doctors advise about eating eggs?

8. What kind of red meat do you prefer? How often do you eat it?

9. What do nutritionists say about eating such foods as bacon, ham, frankfurters, sausage, and cold cuts (baloney, salami, etc.)?

10. Is there any kind of fish or seafood that you prefer? What kind of fish or seafood don't you like? How often during the week do you eat fish or seafood?

11. For you, what should a good salad consist of?

12. What kind of poultry do you eat most often?

13. If you had your choice of eating red meat, poultry, or fish, which would you choose? Why?

14. How often do you eat cheese? What kinds do you prefer? Are there any varieties that you don't like?

15. What are some of your favorite desserts?

16. What do you usually drink with your breakfast? Lunch? Dinner?

17. How often do you eat fast food?

18. What is your favorite ethnic or native food? What does the dish consist of?

HOMEWORK

Part I. Incomplete Dialogues: Using Two-Word Verbs

These dialogues contain words or expressions similar to the two-word verbs introduced in your vocabulary list. In the space provided, write the two-word verb which is closest in meaning to the bold print portion of the statement. Use the past form whenever necessary. When you have completed the dialogues, practice reading them aloud with another student.

go out	take up	take care of
drop by	bring down (S)	warm up (S)
keep down (S)	count on	invite over (S)
try out (S)	feel like	pour over (S)

Example: **A:** Have you been able to **control** your weight as your doctor ordered?
  B: Oh, yes. I've managed to **keep** it **down** by eating low-calorie food.

1. **A:** Did you **heat** the rice before you served it?

   B: I _____ it _____ in the microwave oven.

2. **A:** What time did you **leave the house** this morning?

   B: I _____ _____ at nine.

3. **A:** Would you like to **experiment with** this recipe for lemon pie?

   B: Why not? I like to _____ _____ new recipes.

4. **A:** Grandmother doesn't like it when I **pay** her **an unexpected visit**.

   B: You should always call her before you _____ _____ .

5. **A:** Do you think I can **depend on** Ken to mail the letter for me?

   B: Of course you can _____ _____ him. He's very dependable.

6. **A:** Yesterday, Sally's day was completely **filled with** appointments.

   B: Yes, those interviews certainly _____ _____ all her time, didn't they?

7. **A:** Would you **like** some apple pie?

   B: No, thanks. I really don't _____ _____ having any right now.

8. A: Did you ask the Williamses **to come visit us** tonight?

    B: Yes, I _____ them _____ for dessert

        and coffee.

9. A: Has your husband been able to **lower** his cholesterol count?

    B: Yes, he has. He's _____ it _____ to almost

        normal for his age.

10. A: Who's going to **provide** the refreshments for the party?

    B: The men are going to _____ _____ _____ the drinks,

        and the women will bring the food.

Part II. Vocabulary Building

Following your instructor's directions, use the words and expressions that appear below in sentences or dialogues of your own. Be sure that the meaning of each word or expression is clear in the sentences or dialogues that you write. If a verb has more than one meaning use the meaning used in this lesson.

meal	flavor	do without
recipe	cholesterol	go out
snack	seasoning	drive out
leftovers	take a break *or*	stir up (S)
appetite	coffee break	go over
brunch	*(choose one)*	

> **NOTE:** Of course, you may use additional vocabulary items from this lesson or from previous lessons.

LISTENING COMPREHENSION EXERCISE: STUDENT'S ANSWER SHEET

1. ____ **a)** provide it.

   ____ **b)** taste it.

   ____ **c)** watch it.

2. ____ **a)** contains little fat.

   ____ **b)** is well cut.

   ____ **c)** is clean.

3. ____ **a)** lunch.

   ____ **b)** a light meal.

   ____ **c)** a heavy meal.

4. ____ **a)** crushed into fine particles.

   ____ **b)** cut into pieces.

   ____ **c)** thrown to the ground.

5. ____ **a)** around eleven in the morning.

   ____ **b)** at noon or later.

   ____ **c)** early in the morning.

6. ____ **a)** what spices or condiments to use.

   ____ **b)** the time of the year when it is served.

   ____ **c)** the cooking method used.

7. ____ **a)** You don't like it.

   ____ **b)** It makes no difference one way or the other.

   ____ **c)** You don't want any.

8. ____ **a)** fried chicken.

____ **b)** chicken cut up and broiled.

____ **c)** chicken boiled in a sauce.

9. ____ **a)** I'll make a noise.

____ **b)** I'll call you by telephone.

____ **c)** I'll hit you.

10. ____ **a)** I'll take off on a trip.

____ **b)** I'll have nothing to do.

____ **c)** I'll be busy all day.

CONVERSATION PRACTICE

Using words and expressions you have learned from the vocabulary lists or from the dialogues, choose one of the following situations and with one or two classmates make up a dialogue. Present it to the class according to your instructor's directions. Have at least three exchanges: **A B, A B, A B** or **A B C, A B C, A B C,** depending on which situation you choose.

1. A friend calls you up and asks for the recipe for a particular dish you once served him or her. Tell your friend how to prepare the dish and make suggestions for accompanying (side) dishes. (Your friend should choose a recipe with a few ingredients and/or which is easy to prepare.)

2. You and one or two of your classmates are planning an end-of-the-year party. You plan to invite the other members of the class. Discuss with your partners what dishes you might serve and decide who is to provide what.

3. A friend calls and invites you to dinner at his or her house. You are trying to lose weight and are following a strict diet. Explain the situation to your friend. He or she responds appropriately and you agree to accept the invitation.

4. Call a couple and invite them for brunch or lunch. They are not sure they can make it. Try to convince them by telling them what you plan to serve.

5. You and one or two friends from the office are having a snack and talking about your favorite ethnic foods and restaurants where these foods are served. One of you suggests that you and your friends go to dinner at one of the restaurants some day after work.

Let's Talk About Health and Fitness

DIALOGUES

Read the following dialogues according to the instructions given to you in class. Then answer the questions that follow each dialogue. Take special notice of the boldface vocabulary items used by the speakers. If you don't know the meanings of these words and expressions, you should be able to figure them out from the way the items are used in the dialogues.

1. **A:** Hi, Ross! It's me, Keith, Keith Randall. Don't you remember me?

B: Keith Randall! I didn't recognize you. What happened to you? Don't tell me you went on one of those **fad diets**.

A: Oh, no. I had never been so **out of shape** in my entire life. I was **tired out** all the time—**out of breath**. My clothes didn't **fit** me anymore. Finally, I decided to go in for a **physical**.

B: What did the doctor say?

A: She said I had to **take off** the fifty extra pounds I had **put on**.

B: Wow! You were really **overweight**! Did you **starve** yourself?

A: No, the doctor put me on a **low-calorie** diet. I had to **cut down on** fattening foods—cheeseburgers, French fries. You know, the things I love to eat.

B: And things like ice cream and cake, I bet.

A: Right. I had to **cut out** sweets like that, too.

B: But it's all for the best. You could've **overeaten** until you had a heart attack. How long have you **kept off** that extra weight?

A: About six months. I also started going to a **gym** to **exercise** three nights a week. That helped me **get** back **in shape**. It took me a year to **knock off** the fifty pounds. At first they went fast, and then the last ten were a real **struggle**.

B: Well, congratulations! That's quite an **achievement**. **Keep up** the good work. You look great.

A: And I feel great. Well, I have to **get going**. Good seeing you again.

B: Same here. So long.

Questions

1. Why was it hard for Ross to recognize Keith?

2. What is a fad diet? Can you think of some fad diets you've heard about?

3. How would you describe Keith's appearance before he lost fifty pounds?

4. How did Keith know he was out of shape?

5. Why do you think he decided to see a doctor?

6. What do you think a low-calorie diet consists of?

7. What is another way of saying "cut out sweets"? What exactly do we mean by "sweets"?

8. What's the difference in meaning between **cutting out** certain foods and **cutting down** on them?

9. Before he started dieting, what do you think were some of Keith's other favorite foods?

10. What kind of foods do you think Keith is probably eating now? Name a few of them.

11. How long has it been since Keith and Ross last saw each other? How do you know?

12. What is another way of saying "knock off a few pounds"?

2. A: Excuse me, what time does the next **aerobics** class start?

   B: In ten minutes.

   A: It's the **high-impact** aerobics class, right?

   B: No. It's the **low-impact**. The high-impact is at ten o'clock.

   A: Oh, dear. Now I don't know what to do. I always get the hours mixed up.

   B: Why don't you try this class? The teacher's excellent. She gives lots of **stretching exercises**—the perfect way to **warm up** before **jogging**, running, or even walking. There's no better warm-up.

   A: Well, I guess I'll have to settle for the low-impact. I don't want to **wait around** for an hour. I really need to **unwind**. I'm very tense. You know, **up-tight**.

   B: I started out with high-impact aerobics, but I had to quit because I was overweight. I got too tired and **wore out** very fast. I could never **keep up with** the class. Once I nearly **passed out**. Anyway, I changed to low-impact.

   A: I don't have that problem and doing this kind of exercise helps me **stay fit**. I want to stay **slender**. I need to **burn up** all those extra calories one eats at this time of year! If I **let** myself **go** I'll put on extra pounds and get **flabby** just like that. (Snaps her fingers.)

   B: Oh, here's the teacher. I guess we'll start any moment now. Nice talking to you.

   A: Same here. We'll probably run into each other here again.

Questions

1. Where does the dialogue take place?

2. What's another way of saying "in ten minutes"? What time is it? How do you know?

3. What are aerobic exercises? What is the difference between high-impact and low-impact aerobics?

4. What's the meaning of **warm up** as a verb in this dialogue? What's another meaning of this verb? (See Lesson 8, Dialogue 2.)

5. What does **B** mean by "I need to unwind"?

6. Why did **B** change to low-impact aerobics?

7. What's the meaning of **pass out** here? Compare this with the meaning of the same verb in Lesson 2, Dialogue 1.

8. What's the meaning of the expression **stay fit**?

9. What time of the year does this dialogue take place? Why do you think so?

10. Do you think the people in the dialogue know each other? Are they men or women? Why do you think so?

11. What do you think **A** means by "I'll get flabby"?

3. **A:** I'm frustrated! I'm so **upset**!

B: What's wrong?

A: This is terrible! I can't understand it.

C: Oh, come on. What's happened?

A: I've been **following** my diet **to the letter**. I walk for thirty minutes every day. I swim fifty laps three times a week. And would you believe it? I lost only two pounds this week.

B: Oh, is that all? I thought something awful had happened to you—that you had an accident or something.

C: So did I. You're **making a mountain out of a molehill**. At least you didn't **gain** any weight.

A: But, that's not all. Pat's following the same diet as I am, but he never has time to go walking with me. Yet this morning we weighed ourselves, and he's lost five pounds. Isn't that ridiculous? It doesn't **make sense**.

C: You know something? Somewhere, I read that men **lose weight** faster than women.

B: I'm pretty sure I've read that too.

A: Well, that's what the doctor said, but it still **hurts**. I mean, all the **sacrifices** you make for this.

C: Just look at it this way, if there were a food shortage, and everyone were starving to death, women would outlive us. They just happen to need fewer calories than men.

A: That's no consolation! I still say it's unfair any way you look at it.

B: It sure is.

Questions

1. Why was **A** so upset at the opening of the dialogue?

2. Why were **B** and **C** surprised at **A**'s explanation?

3. What do you think **A** meant when she said she'd been following her diet to the letter?

4. What made **A** even more upset?

5. What do you think "making a mountain out of a molehill" means?

6. Is **C** a man or a woman? How do you know?

7. What explanation does **C** offer to explain **A**'s smaller weight loss compared to Pat's?

8. Is **A** satisfied with **C**'s explanation? What makes you think so?

9. What does **A** mean by "all the sacrifices"? What sort of "sacrifice" do you think she is referring to?

10. What is the meaning of the word **hurt** as it is used in this dialogue?

4. **A:** Hi, Myra.

B: Hi, Sue. How've you been?

A: Much better, thank you.

B: Have you been ill? You've gotten so thin!

A: **Thin**? **Skinny** is the word. I **put** myself **on** a diet because I thought I was too **heavy**. Then after a while I couldn't stop losing weight. I felt so **weak**. So I finally went to a doctor.

B: What happened to you? Did you stop eating?

A: No, but I was slowly killing myself with my crazy diet. The doctor mentioned something called *anorexia nervosa.* She called it an eating disorder.

B: But that could have killed you!

A: So I found out. The doctor said it was a good thing I went to see her when I did. She **put** me **on** a special diet to help my body get back to normal.

B: So what kind of a diet did she put you on? Lots of cake and ice cream, I bet. I'd go for that. I have a terrible **sweet tooth**.

A: No. Nothing like that. She just gave me a sensible balanced diet. She said I have to gain weight and get back in shape as quickly as possible.

B: Well, I hope this diet **builds up** your **strength**. You look so **frail** and you're so **pale**! You're lucky you caught yourself in time. Oh, boy. It's almost ten! I have to go. It was good seeing you and I hope you get back to being your old self real soon. Bye now.

A: Bye.

Questions

1. Is there a difference between being thin or slender and being skinny?

2. Have you heard about *anorexia nervosa* ? Can you tell the class what it is? Do you know anyone who has or has had the disease?

3. What kind of diet do you think **A** had been following before visiting the doctor?

4. What is **B**'s idea of a diet to get **A** back in shape?

5. What is a **sweet tooth**? What do you think are some of **B**'s other favorite foods?

6. What were some ill effects **A** probably suffered from following that "crazy diet"?

7. What does **frail** mean here?

8. What does **pale** mean here?

5. **A:** I'm sorry I have to **call it quits** right here. I can't keep up with you. I have to stop and catch my breath.

B: Are you sure you're OK?

A: Just about. . . . I **give up**! I'm either **out of practice** or I'm **not cut out for** this kind of exercise anymore.

B: Hey, listen, don't forget this is your first time out since you had the flu. Your body is still **picking up the pieces**. Give it a chance.

A: It's amazing what something like the flu can do to you. I mean, I was jogging three miles a day until two weeks ago and look at me now! I'm practically **dead on my feet** and I've hardly jogged a mile. What's the matter with me, anyway?

B: Take it easy. You do look worn out. Let's **sit down** on that bench over there until you **cool down**. You know, you can't suddenly force your body back into action after being sick for two weeks. You have to **work up to** your usual **pace** little by little.

A: Yeah, you're right. But just look at me; I'm **sweating** like a horse.

B: Relax. We'll stay here till you feel better.

A: But I shouldn't **hold** you **back** from getting your exercise. I feel very bad about that.

B: Oh, come on! It's nothing. It could happen to anyone.

A: Thanks, pal. I really appreciate your **thoughtfulness** and **concern**.

Questions

1. Where does the dialogue take place?
2. What are **A** and **B** doing?
3. What is another way of saying "call it quits"?
4. What does **A** mean by "I have to catch my breath"?
5. What does **A** mean by "just about"?
6. What does **A** mean by the expression **I give up**?
7. What does **B** mean by "your body is still picking up the pieces"?
8. How does **B** explain **A**'s problem? How does **A** feel about it?
9. What kind of relationship is there between **A** and **B**?
10. Are the speakers male or female? Explain your answer.

6. **A:** I can't take this any longer. The **stress** here at work is killing me! These people think I'm a machine. All you have to do is just push the right buttons and out comes the printout. No way!

B: Listen, I felt the same way a few months ago, and you know what I did? I started walking at a good pace every day. It's a great way to get rid of **tension**.

A: Yeah. I've heard walking **briskly** is good for you. It really works then?

B: I'm not kidding. It's a great **workout**. Hey, I've got an idea. Why don't we join the health club down the street?

A: Sounds like a great idea, but I don't think it's still open. I heard it was closed.

B: They just changed management and reopened right away.

A: Are you sure?

B: Positive. Look it's only two blocks from here. They have a **fitness room**—with **state-of-the-art** exercising machines, an inside **track** for jogging and walking, and a lot of other facilities. What else can you ask for? And it's so convenient.

A: Forget it! It's probably too expensive.

B: No, I'm sure it's not. Hey, why don't we go find out today? They may have a **package deal**, like two memberships for the price of one. I know some of the other clubs do.

A: What if it's too expensive?

B: What if it's not?

A: OK. You win. Let's have a look at it.

B: Great. Meet you downstairs a little after five. Remember we **get off** early today.

A: OK. See you then.

Questions

1. Where do you think this dialogue takes place?
2. Who might the people talking be? Friends? Officemates? Men? Women? How do you know they don't work on the first floor?
3. Explain in your own words how **A** feels about his or her job?
4. Why do you think jogging or walking would be good for relieving tension?
5. What does **B** mean when he or she says, "I'm not kidding"?
6. What's a **workout**?
7. What excuses does **A** give for not wanting to join the health club? Do you think **B** can persuade **A** to join?
8. What is a health club? What other terms are used for that kind of place?
9. What is meant by the term **state-of-the-art**?
10. What is a package deal? What package deals are you familiar with?

VOCABULARY

All of these words and expressions have been used in the dialogues of this lesson. You have probably been able to tell their meanings from the way they have been used in the dialogues and questions. Although you may not use some of the terms yourself, you should know what they mean when you hear them used by other people.

DIALOGUE 1

fad diet
low-calorie diet
physical (examination)
struggle
achievement

exercise (v)
gym (gymnasium)
fit (v)
starve
overweight
(get) in shape
out of shape

out of breath
tire out (S)
take off (weight, pounds) (S)
put on – add pounds, weight (S)
cut down on
cut out – eliminate
keep off (extra weight) (S)
knock off (S)
keep up (S)
get going
overeat

DIALOGUE 2

aerobics: high-impact, low-impact
stretching exercises
jogging
up-tight
slender
flabby
unwind – wind down, relax
stay fit
warm up (S)
wait around (for)
keep up with
wear out – tire out, become fatigued
pass out
let —— go (S)
burn up (S)

DIALOGUE 3

upset
sacrifice
hurt (v) – cause mental distress, offend
gain (v)
lose (weight)
make sense
follow (something) to the letter
make a mountain out of a molehill

DIALOGUE 4

thin
skinny
heavy
frail
weak
pale
strength
sweet tooth
put —— on (S) – prescribe
build up (S)

DIALOGUE 5

pace (n)
thoughtfulness
concern (n)
sweat (v)
pick up the pieces
dead on (one's) feet
work up to
call it quits
(be) out of practice
(be) cut out for (usually used in the
   negative)
cool down
sit down
hold back (S)
give up (S)

DIALOGUE 6

stress (n)
tension
workout (n)
track (n)
package deal
fitness room
briskly (adj.)
state-of-the-art
get off – finish work

QUESTIONS FOR CLASS DISCUSSION

> **NOTE TO THE INSTRUCTOR:** Select only those questions which are appropriate for your particular class or teaching situation, or for the amount of class time you plan to allow for this activity.

1. Have you ever been on a low-calorie or high-calorie diet? If so, explain what the diet consisted of and what the results of following it were.

2. Do you think you eat a balanced diet? Why do you think so?

3. Do you do any type of exercise? If not, what do you do to stay in shape?

4. What kind of exercise or workout tires you out?

5. What kinds of circumstances could cause a person to be out of breath?

6. What kinds of foods do you love or particularly enjoy eating? Is there any specific time of day when you feel a craving or strong desire for these foods?

7. Have you ever followed a fad diet or a crash diet? If so, what did you eat?

8. Do you take vitamin pills? Which ones? Why do you take those particular pills?

9. How would you describe yourself physically?

10. Have you ever passed out? What were the circumstances?

11. Have you read anything interesting lately about health and fitness? If so, share what you learned with the class.

12. In your culture, has the idea of being healthy and fit become important recently? If so, how have the lifestyles of people in your culture changed?

HOMEWORK

Part I. Incomplete Dialogues Using Two-Word Verbs

These dialogues contain words or expressions similar to the two-word verbs introduced in the dialogues of this lesson. In the space provided, write the two-word verb which is closest in meaning to the boldface portion of the statement. Be sure to use the correct form. When you have completed the dialogues, practice reading them aloud, preferably together with another person.

pass out	put on (S)	warm up (S)
tire out	take off (S)	cool down
cut out (S)	cut down on	cheer up (S)
keep up	burn up	come up with

Example: **A:** Jane **suggested** a great idea for our class party.
  B: She always **comes up with** something original.

1. **A:** What kinds of food did you **eliminate** when you went on a low-calorie diet?

   B: I _____ _____ fried foods and sweets.

2. **A:** How much weight did John **gain** last summer?

   B: He _____ _____ twenty pounds.

3. **A:** Have you ever **fainted**?

   B: Yes, once I _____ _____ after gym class.
   I guess I exercised too much.

4. **A:** Now that the holiday parties are over, I'd better exercise to **lose** some extra pounds right away.

   B: How about walking briskly for an hour every day for a few days? That's how I
   _____ _____ my extra weight last Christmas.

5. **A:** What do you do to **refresh** yourself after playing tennis?

   B: I _____ _____ by drinking lots and lots of water.

6. **A:** I'm **exhausted**. How do you feel?

   B: I'm also _____ _____ .

7. **A:** How do many athletes **get ready** for competitions?

   B: They _____ _____ by exercising right before they participate.

8. **A:** If you want to get in shape you have to **eat less of** those foods you love.

   B: I know. I'm trying to _____ _____ _____ them.

9. **A:** Come on! Don't feel so bad! **Be happy**. Losing a tennis match isn't the end of the world.

   B: You want me to _____ _____ after I played so badly?

10. **A:** If you **continue** dieting you'll be in shape in no time at all.

    B: I hope I can _____ it _____ till I reach my goal.

Part II. Vocabulary Building

Following your instructor's directions, use ten of the words and expressions that appear below in sentences or dialogues of your own. Be sure that the meaning of each word or expression is clear in the sentences or dialogues that you write. *When a word has more than one meaning, choose the meaning used in this lesson.*

gain weight, lose weight *(choose one)*
diet, low-calorie diet *(choose one)*
sweet tooth
out of practice
take off (weight) (S)
put on (weight) (S)
fit (adj.)
warm up (v)

physical (n) *or* physical examination
out of breath
aerobics
overweight
wait around (for)
hold back (S)
wear out

NOTE: Of course, you may also use other vocabulary items from this or from previous lessons.

LISTENING COMPREHENSION EXERCISE: STUDENT'S ANSWER SHEET

1. ____ **a)** has a particular body build.

    ____ **b)** is below normal weight.

    ____ **c)** is in good physical condition.

2. ____ **a)** go to an air-conditioned room.

    ____ **b)** rest a few minutes.

    ____ **c)** drink something cold.

3. ____ **a)** didn't like the game.

    ____ **b)** wasn't allowed to play the game.

    ____ **c)** didn't have a special talent for the game.

4. ____ **a)** get some air.

    ____ **b)** lose weight.

    ____ **c)** do something relaxing.

5. ____ **a)** She's dying.

    ____ **b)** She's very tired.

    ____ **c)** Her feet hurt.

6. ____ **a)** It's not easy.

    ____ **b)** It's not difficult.

    ____ **c)** It's not logical.

7. ____ **a)** It's the most highly developed.

    ____ **b)** It's concerned with the arts.

    ____ **c)** It's owned by the state.

8. _____ **a)** stop eating meat.

_____ **b)** eat chopped meat.

_____ **c)** eat less meat.

9. _____ **a)** I get tired.

_____ **b)** I warm up.

_____ **c)** I start out fast.

10. _____ **a)** I've gained weight.

_____ **b)** I've lost weight.

_____ **c)** I've maintained my weight.

CONVERSATION PRACTICE

Using words and expressions you have learned from the vocabulary used in the dialogues of this lesson, choose one of the following situations, and with a classmate make up a dialogue in which each person speaks three times. Present it to the class according to your instructor's directions.

1. You are walking down the street and a person walks over and greets you. You realize it is a friend you have not seen for some time. This person looks very well but has lost a lot of weight since you last saw him or her. Greet your friend and inquire about the weight loss. Congratulate your friend on his or her appearance and say goodbye in an appropriate manner.

2. You are visiting a friend who tells you that he or she is out of shape and asks for some advice. You give your friend some tips for getting back in shape and he or she accepts your suggestions.

3. You are walking or jogging with a friend. You suddenly realize that your partner looks ill. You stop and inquire about his or her health. Depending on what your friend tells you, you decide whether to continue walking or jogging.

4. Your friend decides he or she is going to follow a new diet which claims to help a person lose twenty pounds in one week. (You and your partner decide what this diet will consist of.) You listen to your friend and then try to convince him or her not to go on that fad diet because it could be dangerous to his or her health. You try to convince your friend to try a sensible, low-calorie diet. Your friend agrees to try the diet you suggest.

 10

Let's Talk About Being Sick

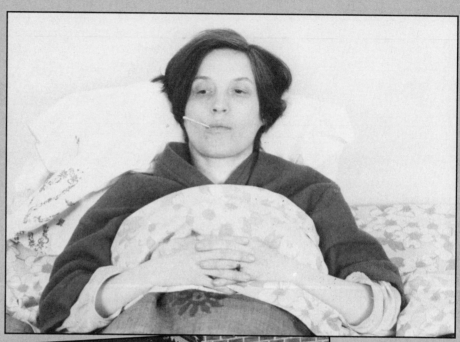

MYONG CHOI, M.D.
RADIOLOGY X-선과

I. VILLALON, M.D.

FRANCIS ESQUERRE, M.D.

PEDRO CHOY, M.D.

JULIO ARMINAN, M.D.

CESAR TORRAS, M.D.

EMILE SOMEKH, M.D.
ALLERGY

FRANCISCO PEREDA, M.D.

KUNCHUL YOON, M.D.

BENJAMIN PAGOVICH, M.D.

GERARDO MACHADO, M.D.
PEDIATRICIAN

ALEJANDRO URRUTIA, M.D.

AUGUSTO MOREANO, M.D.

IGLESIAS, M.D.

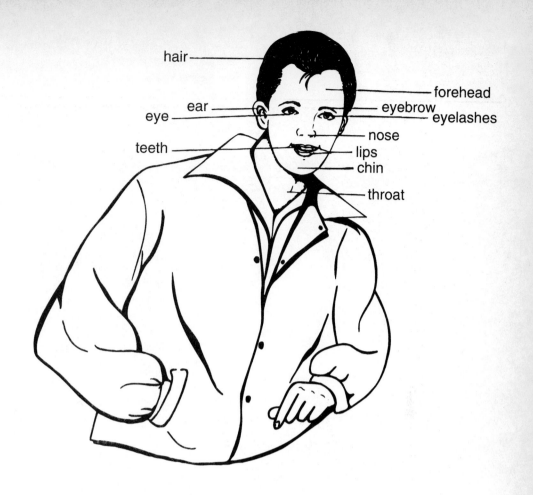

hair — forehead — eyebrow — eyelashes — ear — eye — nose — teeth — lips — chin — throat

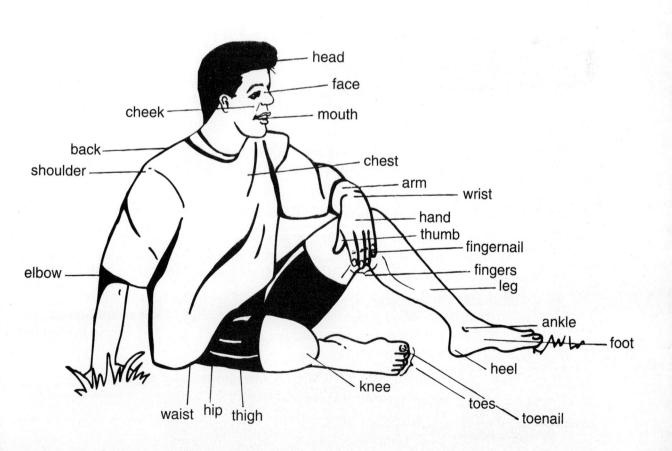

head — face — cheek — mouth — back — shoulder — chest — arm — wrist — hand — thumb — fingernail — fingers — leg — elbow — ankle — foot — heel — waist — hip — thigh — knee — toes — toenail

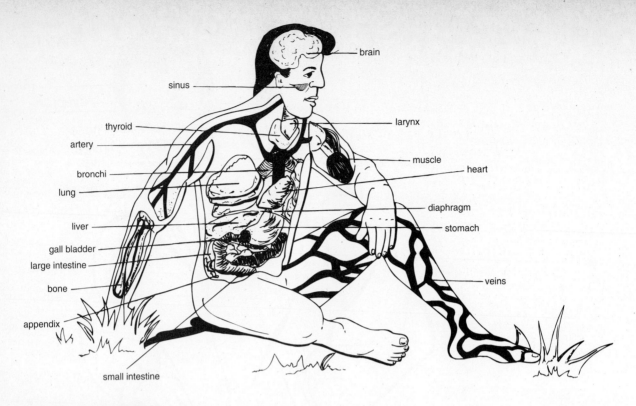

brain
sinus
thyroid
artery
bronchi
lung
liver
gall bladder
large intestine
bone
appendix
small intestine
larynx
muscle
heart
diaphragm
stomach
veins

DIALOGUES

In studying these dialogues, pay particular attention to the boldface words and phrases. You are not expected to be able to use all of them, but you should be familiar with them so that you will understand when you hear another speaker use them.

1. **A:** Good morning, Mrs. Bradford. This is Tom Benton.

   B: Oh, good morning, Tom. Is there something wrong? You sound **nervous**.

   A: I just wanted to let you know that Miriam won't be coming in to work for a while. She was **operated on** for appendicitis yesterday morning.

   B: Oh, my heavens! Is she all right?

   A: She's fine, thank God! When I left the hospital last night she was **sitting up** in bed. Her **surgeon** told her that today she should **get out of** bed and **walk around** a bit. She's still **in** a lot of **pain**.

   B: How long will she be **hospitalized**? I'd like to send her some flowers.

   A: Thank you. That's very kind of you. She'll be there only a day or two. The doctor said he'll probably **discharge** her tomorrow or the day after. Of course, then she'll have to **rest up** at home for a while. She'll have to take a short **sick leave**.

   B: Well, thank God she **came through** it all right. Please give her my regards and tell her not to worry about being away from the office. She's **accumulated** a lot of **sick days** and she might as well use some of them. I'll try to stop by the hospital this afternoon or tonight.

   A: Thank you, Mrs. Bradford. I'll tell Miriam. I'm sure she'll **be up and about** in no time. The doctor says she's in excellent shape for a woman of her age. Goodbye.

   B: Goodbye, Tom. Thanks for calling.

Questions

1. What is the relationship between Mrs. Bradford and Miriam? How can you tell?
2. What is the relationship between Tom Benton and Miriam?
3. What does the word **discharge** mean in this dialogue?
4. What did Mrs. Bradford mean when she said, "she came through it all right"?
5. What does a doctor who is a surgeon specialize in?
6. What is a **sick day**?
7. What is **sick leave**?
8. How do you know that Miriam is not a young woman?
9. What's another way of saying "she'll be up and about in no time"?
10. What do we mean when we say a person is in "excellent shape"?

2. **A:** Good morning, Brenda. My heavens! What's the matter with you? Your eyes are all **puffed up** and your nose is all red. Is it from a cold or do you have an **allergy**?

B: An allergy. I feel absolutely awful. I'm very **allergic** to dust and there's a lot of construction going on in my neighborhood. I **sneezed** and **coughed** all night. I hardly slept at all.

A: No wonder you look so **washed-out**. Hasn't your **allergist prescribed** any **medication**?

B: Yes. I always **take a pill** twice a day—when I get up, and before I go to bed. The trouble is—I ran out of the pills my doctor gave me the day before yesterday.

A: Well, can't you get the **prescription refilled**?

B: Yes, but I'm due for my monthly **shot** this afternoon. I'm going to ask him for something stronger. The **antihistamine** he gave me the last time doesn't seem to be doing me much good.

A: Well, take it easy today. I hope you feel better tomorrow.

B: Thanks, professor. I hope so too. I have a math test.

Questions

1. What's another way of saying "your eyes are puffed up"?
2. What does **B** mean by "I hardly slept at all"?
3. What does the expression **washed-out** mean in this dialogue?
4. What's another word for **shot** as it is used in this dialogue?
5. What does **B** mean when he or she says the medicine doesn't seem to be doing much good? (Refer to Lesson 3, Dialogue 3.)
6. How do you know that **B**'s doctor is a man?
7. Give two reasons why you know that **B** is a student.

3. **A:** Hi, Bill. Haven't seen you in **quite a while**. How're you enjoying your **retirement**?

B: Not very much right now. I've been **feeling under the weather** lately, and I don't know what's the matter—I'm not really sick, but I don't exactly feel well either. No pep, no energy, no ambition.

A: Have you had a **checkup** lately? Maybe you should see a doctor.

B: I went last week. She **checked** me **over pretty thoroughly**. She said I'm in good shape—just need to **keep busy** and get more exercise. That's why you see me out walking. How're *you* doing? Is that hip of yours **bothering** you again? I noticed you're **limping** a little.

A: Not much—only when I forget to **take** my **medicine**. Then my **arthritis acts up**, especially in this damp weather we've been having lately. Otherwise, I feel **pretty good**. I manage to **get around** OK. Well, it was nice talking to you. Take care.

B: You too. So long now.

Questions

1. What's another way of saying **in quite a while**?
2. How do you know that the speakers are not young?
3. From the way it is used in this dialogue can you tell the meaning of the expression **to feel under the weather**?
4. What does the verb **check over** mean in this dialogue?
5. In this dialogue, what do the expressions **pretty thoroughly** and **pretty good** mean?
6. What's another word for **thoroughly**?
7. What are some of the ways a retired person could keep busy?
8. In what part of the body does **A** have arthritis? Can you explain what arthritis is?
9. What does **A** mean by saying that his or her arthritis has been acting up?
10. How do you know that the area where **A** and **B** live has been having a lot of rain lately?
11. What does **A** mean by "I manage to get around OK"?
12. What other physical problems or injuries could cause a person to limp?
13. What does the word **bother** mean as it is used in this dialogue?

4. **A:** Alice told me your daughter is in the hospital. I hope it isn't anything serious.

B: It was *very* serious. She almost died. She had **viral pneumonia**. For a while it was **touch and go**. We didn't know whether she'd **make it** or not. But, thank God, she **pulled through**, and now she's doing just fine. Of course, she's still very weak.

A: I'm sorry to hear that she was so sick. But how did a big strong girl like Janet get a **serious illness** like pneumonia?

B: She **caught a bad cold** jogging in that cold rainy weather we had a while back. Instead of staying home and taking it easy, she **kept going**, and the cold kept getting worse. She couldn't **get rid of** it. She developed **bronchitis** and then the **infection** spread to her lungs.

A: Well, I'm certainly glad she's **recuperating** so nicely. How much longer will she have to stay in the hospital?

B: She's coming home tomorrow, but it's going to take a while for her to **get over** this thing. She'll have to build up her strength before she can go back to school.

A: Well, please give her my best regards. Tell her to take care of herself so she can get well quickly.

B: Thanks, David. I will.

Questions

1. Look at **B**'s answer to **A**'s first question. Express the idioms **touch and go**, **make it**, and **pull through** in your own words.

2. What does "she kept going" mean in this dialogue?

3. What organs of the body would be affected by pneumonia?

4. What is a synonym for **recuperate**?

5. What does the verb **get over** mean in this dialogue? (You learned another meaning of the word in Lesson 5, Dialogue 1.)

6. Who might David be? Who might Alice be?

5. **A:** Hi, Jamie. Just calling to say hello. How are you anyway?

B: Oh, Connie. I've got a terrible cold. I sneezed all night. I have such a **runny nose**, I've **used up** a whole box of tissues already.

A: Join the club! I'm just getting over a horrible cold myself. My nose is still **stuffed up**, and I've got a bad **cough**, especially at night. Are you taking anything?

B: So far, no. I just **came down with** it last night. Before that I had the **sniffles**, and my nose was **itchy**, and I had a sore throat, but I didn't have a real cold. But last night it really hit me.

A: All the typical symptoms. Are you drinking plenty of liquids?

B: Yes, but I'm going to take **aspirin** and **stay in bed** for a couple of days. I've learned from experience that it's the quickest way to get rid of a bad cold.

A: I know what! I'll make some chicken soup and **bring** it **over**. That was always my mother's favorite **remedy** for colds when we were kids.

B: Oh, Connie, that sounds wonderful! I've had so much fruit juice I'm about to float away. Chicken soup would be a nice change.

A: OK. I'll **be over** this afternoon. Take care—and stay in bed.

B: Bye. See you in a little while.

Questions

1. What's a runny nose?

2. What did Connie mean when she told Jamie to "join the club"?

3. How do you breathe when your nose is stuffed up?

4. What does Jamie mean when she says, "it (the cold) really hit me"?

5. How do you know that Jamie (**B**) has had colds before?

6. What is another word for **remedy**? What is the remedy in this dialogue?

7. How do you know that Jamie likes chicken soup?

6. **A:** Hello. How are you? Where have you been? I haven't seen you for quite a while. What's wrong with your face? You're all **broken out**!

B: You won't believe this! I've had the **chickenpox**!

A: Chickenpox! I thought only kids got that.

B: So did I. You know there was an **epidemic** in our school. Well, several of the children in my kindergarten class **were out** sick with it. So naturally I was **exposed to** it. I guess that's how I caught it.

A: I've never had chickenpox. What are the **symptoms**? I know it's very **contagious**, but I didn't realize adults could get it.

B: I had a bad headache and then I felt **dizzy** and unsteady on my feet. I seemed to be very weak. I took my temperature and found out I had a **fever.** I thought I was coming down with the **flu**. But then I started to **break out**. Pretty soon I was covered with a red **rash**.

A: How awful! **Are** you **over** it? I won't catch it from you, will I?

B: No, I'm not contagious anymore. I'm over the worst of it now. The rash has **cleared up** mostly.

A: Well, take it easy. I hope you get over it completely soon. I'll call you to see how you're doing. When you **feel up to** it, we can go out to lunch on a Saturday.

B: OK. That would be fun. Call me in about a week. I'll see you.

Questions

1. How do you know that **B** is a teacher?

2. What do we mean when we talk about the **symptoms** of a disease?

3. What do we mean when we say a disease is **contagious**? Can you mention some other contagious diseases?

4. What does **A** mean by "are you over it?"

5. What word could you use instead of **catch** in this dialogue?

6. What does **clear up** mean here?

7. What does the expression to **feel up to** mean in this dialogue?

8. Why do you think **A** suggests having lunch on a Saturday instead of a weekday?

9. Compare the meaning of **be over** in this dialogue with the meaning of the same verb in Dialogue 5.

7. **A:** (Sneezing.) A-a-a-chooo! A-a-a-chooo! A-a-a-a-chooooo!

B: God bless you! Why are you **sniffling**? Don't you have a **tissue** to **wipe your nose**?

A: No. I didn't bring a purse with me. Do you have any tissues with you?

B: Of course. I always carry a package of tissues. Here, help yourself.

A: Thanks, Mom. I hope I'm not coming down with a cold. The senior orchestra **auditions** are **coming up** next week. I won't be able to play if I have to keep **blowing my nose** every two minutes.

B: Well, you should try to go to bed early tonight. Maybe you just have the sniffles from the cold air-conditioning in this place.

Questions

1. What excuse does **A** give for not having a tissue?

2. How do you know that **A** is **B**'s daughter?

3. How do you know that **A** plays a musical instrument?

4. About how old do you think **A** is? Why do you think so? (There's a clue in this dialogue.)

5. Where do you think the conversation might be taking place?

VOCABULARY

All of these words and expressions have been used in the dialogues of this lesson. You probably have been able to tell their meanings from the way in which they have been used in the various dialogues and questions.

DIALOGUE 1

nervous
surgeon
hospitalize
sick leave, sick days
be in pain
be up and about
operate on
sit up
discharge
walk around
rest up
get out of (bed)
come through – to endure something
   successfully

DIALOGUE 2

allergy; allergic; allergist
sneeze
cough
medication
washed out – tired-looking
prescribe; prescription
antihistamine
take a pill
refill
shot – injection
puff up

DIALOGUE 3

retirement
checkup
arthritis
pretty – quite, very
pretty good
thoroughly
limp
feel under the weather
keep busy
take medicine
quite a while
bother (v) – cause pain
act up
get around
check over (S)

DIALOGUE 4

viral pneumonia
bronchitis
infection
serious illness
recuperate
catch a cold
touch and go
keep going
pull through – survive
get rid of
get over – recuperate, get well
make it – survive

DIALOGUE 5

runny nose
stuffed up – stopped up, filled with
    something (mucous)

sniffles
remedy
aspirin
itchy
cough (n)
stay in bed
use up (S)
come down with
bring over (S)
be over – come by, visit

DIALOGUE 6

chickenpox
epidemic
symptoms
contagious
rash
flu – influenza
fever
dizzy
break out
be exposed to
be over – no longer sick
be out – absent (because of sickness)
feel up to
clear up

DIALOGUE 7

sniff (v)
tissue – facial tissue
audition
blow (one's) nose
wipe (one's) nose
come up – scheduled

QUESTIONS FOR CLASS DISCUSSION

1. Do you have any allergies? If so, what substances are you allergic to? Do you take any medication for your allergy?

2. When you feel under the weather, do you stay at home and take it easy or do you try to keep going?

3. Have you ever had any contagious disease? Which one(s)? What were the symptoms?

4. Have you or has any member of your family ever had a serious illness? Can you tell us about it?

5. Is influenza (the flu) a common ailment in your culture?

6. When someone in your family is sick, who usually takes care of that person?

7. When a family member is hospitalized, do other family members go to the hospital to care for him or her or is that person left to be cared for by the nurses in the hospital?

8. Does your mother, grandmother or someone else in your family have a favorite remedy for an illness such as a common cold?

9. In some cultures, folk medicine is very important. Can you think of any examples of folk medicine in your culture?

10. Do you have your own personal remedy for getting rid of a cold?

11. In some cultures, there are superstitions about certain illnesses or diseases. Can you think of any in your culture?

12. What sorts of epidemics break out in your country? Do they usually break out among children or among the general public?

13. Have you ever had to have an operation?

14. Are there any particular seasons of the year when you tend to get sick with a cold or an allergy?

15. Do you have a family physician? For what sort of illness would you go to him or her?

HOMEWORK

Part I. Using Two-Word Verbs and Idioms

In the following dialogues you are to fill in the blank spaces in the answer part with the *past tense form* of the verb. All these verbs have been used in the dialogues of this lesson.

1. **A:** When did you **run out of** your cough medicine?

    B: I _____ _____ _____ it just last night.

2. **A:** How long ago did the epidemic of chickenpox **break out**?

    B: It _____ _____ about two weeks ago.

3. **A:** Is Jack able to **sit up** in bed yet?

    B: Oh, yes. He _____ _____ for a few hours yesterday.

4. **A:** Did you remember to **take** a vitamin pill this morning?

    B: Yes, I _____ _____ before breakfast.
                         (Use a pronoun.)

5. **A:** When did Jack's cold **get worse?**

    B: It _____ worse over the weekend.

Part II. Vocabulary Building

According to your instructor's directions, use ten or more of the following vocabulary items in sentences or dialogues of your own. You may use more than one of the items in one sentence or dialogue. However, you must write at least ten sentences or five dialogues. *Be sure to use the items with the same meanings as those used in this lesson.* Underline the vocabulary items.

epidemic
disease
contagious
allergic; allergy *(choose one)*
infection
dizzy
prescription
take medicine, take a pill *(choose one)*

remedy
blow (one's) nose
get better
get over, get well
get around
pull through
act up
operate on

LISTENING COMPREHENSION EXERCISE: STUDENT'S ANSWER SHEET

Part I

1. ____ **a)** I'd rather eat at home.

____ **b)** I'm not well enough yet.

____ **c)** I don't have any appetite yet.

2. ____ **a)** He's not feeling as well as he usually does.

____ **b)** He's fine but he doesn't like the weather.

____ **c)** The weather makes him feel sick.

3. ____ **a)** He's getting worse.

____ **b)** He's getting tired.

____ **c)** He's getting well.

4. ____ **a)** I feel silly.

____ **b)** I'm unsteady on my feet.

____ **c)** I'm tired of standing up.

5. ____ **a)** He gave me a complete examination.

____ **b)** He passed me along to another doctor.

____ **c)** He asked me to pay him by check.

Part II

1. ____ **a)** I went to buy some.

____ **b)** I used all of them.

____ **c)** I threw them away.

2. ____ **a)** I'm getting a cold.

____ **b)** I'm getting over a cold.

____ **c)** I'm taking care of a cold.

3. ____ **a)** survived it.

____ **b)** died from it.

____ **c)** avoided it.

4. ____ **a)** ends.

____ **b)** continues.

____ **c)** occurs.

5. ____ **a)** is getting better.

____ **b)** is painful.

____ **c)** is not bothering me.

CONVERSATION PRACTICE

With a classmate, choose one of the following situations and work out a conversation. After you have worked it out and practiced it, present your dialogue to the class according to your instructor's directions. Be sure to choose words and expressions from the vocabulary items used in this lesson. Each dialogue should have at least three exchanges: **A B, A B, A B**.

1. **A** is sneezing and coughing and blowing his or her nose. **B** notices **A**'s condition and the two of them discuss the symptoms and probable or possible consequences.

2. You, **A**, and a friend, **B**, hear that another friend, **C**, has been hospitalized for an operation. (You and your friend decide what the operation is for.) Discuss **C**'s condition as to how long he or she will have to remain in the hospital, whether you should visit him or her or send flowers, and so on.

3. Your friend's parents are retired and living in a warm climate. Ask your friend about his or her parents' health. Use idioms from this lesson to describe their condition.

4. There is an epidemic of a childhood disease in the school where one of you teaches. (You and your partner decide which disease.) Discuss the situation and the effect of the epidemic on that person.

5. A friend invites you to a party but you are not feeling well. (You decide what is wrong with you.) Explain to your friend why you can't accept the invitation.

6. With one or two classmates, think up a situation of your own that is similar to one in this lesson and work up a dialogue about it using appropriate vocabulary items.

11

Let's Talk About Clothes

CLOTHES

dress

sleeveless blouse

short-sleeved blouse

polo shirt

T shirt

turtleneck sweater

cardigan sweater

jacket

jeans

coat

raincoat

jogging suit

tights

shorts

swimsuit

swim trunks

bikini

bathrobe

pajamas

nightgown

FOOTWEAR

boots

low-heeled pumps

thongs

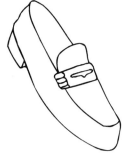
slippers

oxfords

loafers

high-heeled pumps

flats

sandals

athletic shoes

UNDERWEAR AND HOSIERY

jockey shorts

boxer shorts

panties

brassiere

slip

half slip

stockings

pantyhose

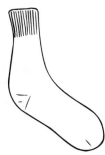
socks

athletic socks

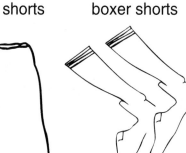

Questions

1. What's the difference between a **shopping mall** and a **shopping center**?
2. Since Alice saw Pat, why do you think she didn't speak to her?
3. How do you know that Pat drove to the shopping mall?
4. What do you think Alice means by "great buys"? What are **special** sales?
5. What does the word **material** mean in this dialogue? Can you think of another word which means the same thing?
6. Why didn't Alice buy the dress?
7. What does "it was reduced 40 percent" mean?
8. Why does Pat prefer clothes that are wash-and-wear?

8. **A:** Why are you wearing a **heavy, long-sleeved sweatshirt** on a day like today? Why don't you **take** it **off** and **put on** something **lighter**?

   B: I was just about to **change into** something **cooler**. But I have to take a shower first. I'm looking for my orange **T-shirt**. I **washed** it **out** last night and **hung** it **up** in the bathroom to dry but it's not there. Do you know what happened to it?

   A: You mean that **sleeveless tank top**? It was dry, so I **folded** it **up** and put it in your drawer. Hurry up and **get dressed**. I'm going to the **shopping center**, and I want you to go with me to help me **pick out** a present for Aunt Bess.

   B: OK. I'll be ready in a few minutes.

Questions

1. Who do you think the speakers are?
2. What kind of day do you think it is? How can you tell?
3. Why do you think **B** was wearing a sweatshirt?
4. What do the words **heavy** and **light** mean when used to refer to clothes?
5. What's the difference between a **sweatshirt**, a **T-shirt**, and a **tank top**?
6. What's the difference in meaning between **get dressed** and **get dressed up**?

9. **A:** I like this suit. It's exactly what I've been **looking for**. Fits me well, too, except the pants are a little **loose** around the **waist** and the sleeves need **shortening**. Can you **alter** it for me?

   B: I'm sorry, sir. We don't **make alterations** on sale **merchandise**. But I can give you the name of a **tailor** who'll do it for you—very reasonably. He's right around the corner in the next block. I have his card right here.

   A: OK. I'll take the suit. Can I pay by check?

   B: Yes, sir. Do you have some identification with your picture on it?

   A: Is a driver's license OK?

   B: That'll be fine. You can pay the cashier. Thank you and come again.

Questions

1. How do you know the customer is a man?
2. What does the customer mean when he says that the pants are a little loose?
3. How do you know that the sleeves are too long?
4. What does the expression **make alterations** mean?
5. How do you know that the suit is being sold at a reduced price?
6. What is **merchandise**?
7. What kind of a card is the salesperson talking about? What information would this type of card contain?

10. **A:** Harry's always so **well-groomed**. He's always **up on** the latest **trends** in **menswear**. He must spend a lot of money on his clothes.

B: No, I don't think he does. Jack, you don't have to wear expensive clothes or the latest **fashion** to be well-groomed. You just have to **be** carefully **dressed** and make sure your clothes are clean and **neat**—and keep your shoes polished.

A: Yeah, I guess maybe you're right about that. It doesn't matter what kind of clothes you're wearing. You can even be well-groomed in neat-looking blue jeans and a clean **polo shirt**.

Questions

1. What does Jack mean when he says that Harry is up on the latest trends?
2. Do you agree or disagree with **B**'s definition of being well-groomed?
3. Does **A** agree completely with that definition?
4. Do you agree with *his* definition of being well-groomed?
5. What does being **well-groomed** mean when applied to a woman?

11. **A:** Good morning, sir. Is anyone helping you?

B: No, thanks. I'm just looking.

A: Is there anything in particular you're looking for?

B: Not really. I'm just **killing time** while I **wait for** my wife. She has a business meeting next door.

A: I see. We're having a special sale on **sports slacks**—30 percent off. Would you like to look at them?

B: Might as well. Let me see what you have—nothing too flashy. Thirty-four waist, thirty-three long.

A: Yes, sir. They're right over there on the rack behind you. I'm sure you'll find something you'll like.

B: (After looking for a minute or two.) These two **pairs** look pretty good. Where can I try them on?

A: The **dressing rooms** are to your left—at the end of the counter.

B: (After a few minutes.) The yellow pair fits very well, but the blue one is too **tight**.

A: Would you like to try on a larger size or a different style?

B: No, thanks. I'll settle for these.

A: How about a **sport shirt** to go with them? We also have a special on shirts.

B: OK. Show me what you have in a **short sleeve** in medium. I don't want any loud colors, now.

A: Yes, sir. Right over here.

B: (Pointing.) How about that one up there ?

A: Oh, I'm sorry, sir. That one's not **for sale**. It's just for display.

B: Oh, well. Let me see that one with the yellow and blue **stripes.** Is this a medium?

A: Yes, sir. That yellow will go very well with the pants. You'll have a **nice-looking** outfit. Yellow is very **fashionable** this season.

B: OK. I'll take it. Where can I pay for these things? Do you take credit cards?

A: Yes, we do. You can pay the cashier to your left. How about some **socks?** Or a **belt**, perhaps?

B: No, thanks. That'll be all. I didn't intend to **do** any **shopping** when I came in here. I was just **killing time**. Here's my wife now. Hi, honey. (They walk to the cashier's desk.) How was the meeting?

C: Uh-h-h-h. Don't ask. It was a complete **waste of time**. I'll tell you about it later. Well! I see you didn't **waste** your **time**. What did you buy?

B: Oh, just a pair of slacks and a sport shirt. They were on sale.

C: (They walk away from the cashier's desk.) Did he give you the **receipt**?

B: Yeah. Here it is. Come on. Let's get something to eat. I'm **starved**.

C: Good idea. They didn't even offer us a cup of coffee, and I didn't have any breakfast.

Questions

1. When a customer says he is "just looking," what does he really mean?

2. Is the man who is shopping tall? Short? Of medium height? Is he fat? Thin? How can you tell?

3. About how old do you think he might be? What makes you think so?

4. What can you say about his taste in clothes?

5. What do you think the customer means by "loud" colors?

6. During what season does this dialogue take place? What makes you think so?

7. What can you say about the salesperson?

8. Can you tell anything about the wife from her conversation?

9. What does the expression **I'm starved** really mean? During what part of the day does this conversation take place? How do you know?

10. What's the difference in meaning between **for sale** and **on sale**?

11. What's the difference in meaning between a **recipe**, a **prescription**, and a **receipt**? (Incidentally, the letter **p** in the word **receipt** is silent.)

12. What's the difference in meaning between to **kill time** and to **waste time**?

VOCABULARY

DIALOGUE 1

tennis shoes
toes (of a shoe)
sole (of a shoe)
find the time
wear well
hard wear
wear out (S) – become unusable
fall apart

DIALOGUE 2

suit
tie
size
shop (v)
good-looking
have an eye for
on sale
take with (S)

DIALOGUE 3

outfit
handbag
earrings
blouse
skirt
set
match (v)
shade (of color)
be becoming
go well with
have on – wear
go with – match, go together

DIALOGUE 4

pull-on pants
pre-teen
shipment
material – fabric
beige
light (color)
dark (color)
machine-washable
cóme in* – be available, obtainable
come ín – arrive
stop in

DIALOGUE 5

sweater
tag
sales slip
credit voucher
refund slip
cashier
full amount
just in case
hand-washable
fade
shrink, shrank
exchange
give back (S)

DIALOGUE 6

cocktail dress
rack
price tag
lower-priced
run – cost, sell for
out of stock
in stock

---

* Remember: here the stress is on the word **come.**

DIALOGUE 7

shopping mall
sales
discount
window shopping
label
wrinkle (v)
reduced
dry clean
wash-and-wear
iron (v)
take advantage of
go shopping
stay open
try on (S)

DIALOGUE 8

sweatshirt
T-shirt
tank top
shopping center
long-sleeved
sleeveless
heavy
light (lighter)
cool (color)
take off (S)
put on (S)
get dressed
change into
wash out (S)
hang up (S)
fold up (S)
pick out (S)

DIALOGUE 9

waist
tailor
merchandise
alter
make alterations
loose
shorten
look for

DIALOGUE 10

menswear
trends
fashion
polo shirt
neat
well-groomed
be up on (something)
be dressed

DIALOGUE 11

sport slacks
sport shirt
short sleeve
socks
belt
receipt
pair (of pants)
stripes
dressing room
tight
fashionable
nice-looking
for sale
kill time
waste time
waste of time
do shopping
wait for

QUESTIONS FOR CLASS DISCUSSION

> **NOTE TO THE INSTRUCTOR:** Choose only those questions which are appropriate to your particular classroom situation or to the culture in which you are teaching. Some of the questions could use up a considerable amount of class time.

1. *(For the women.)* Which colors do you think are most becoming to you?

2. *(For the men.)* Which colors do you think you look best in?

3. Do you like to dress up? For what occasions?

4. How important to you is keeping up with the latest fashions?

5. Are you a conformist? That is, do you like to wear the same styles, colors, accessories, etc., that your friends wear, or do you prefer to "do your own thing" (be a nonconformist)? Explain.

6. If you have an article of clothing that you particularly like, do you continue to wear it even though it may be considered out of style?

7. What do you do with your clothes if you are tired of them and no longer want to wear them even though they are not worn out?

8. Mention three occasions when you think it is important for someone to be well-dressed.

9. How important is it to you whether your best friend (or spouse) is well-groomed?

10. *(For the women in the class.)* Do you ever read fashion magazines or attend fashion shows?

11. How old were you when you first began to choose your own clothes?

12. When you shop for clothes, do you prefer to go alone or to have someone go with you? Explain your answer.

13. Have you ever bought something just because you liked it and it was on sale and since then never have worn it? If so, why?

14. About what percent of your monthly income (or allowance) do you spend on clothes?

15. When you are shopping for clothes and find something you like, do you look at the price tag before you decide whether to buy the item? Why?

16. Do you like to wear T-shirts with messages printed on them?

17. Can you mention any unusual messages you've seen printed on T-shirts?

18. What do you usually do with your clothes when you take them off? Hang them up? Fold them? Throw them on the bed or a chair? Hang them on a doorknob?

19. Do you like to receive articles of clothing as gifts, or do you prefer to choose your own things?

20. Do you like to wear jewelry? Do you ever buy expensive jewelry for yourself or do you prefer to receive it as a gift?

21. Do you have a particular fondness for certain articles of clothing and therefore buy a lot of them (shoes, ties, scarves, etc.)?

HOMEWORK

Part I. Incomplete Dialogues Using Two-Word Verbs

These dialogues contain some of the two-word verbs used in this lesson. Some of the verbs have irregular past-tense forms; others have regular *-ed* endings. In completing the dialogues be sure to use the correct present- or past-tense form. Also, most of the verbs are separable and require an object between the two parts. In those sentences, use pronouns in your answer, either singular or plural, according to the object. When you have completed the dialogues, practice reading them aloud with a friend. Try to guess who the speakers might be in each of the dialogues.

Example: **A:** Did they **give** you **back** your money when you returned the dress?
              B: Yes, they **gave** me **back** the full amount with no problem.

1. **A:** Why did you **take off** your jacket? It's cold in here.

   B: I _____ _____ _____ because it was wet. I got caught
                         (pronoun)
   in the rain.

2. **A:** Kids sure **wear out** their tennis shoes fast these days, don't they?

   B: They sure do! Ken _____ _____ _____ in six weeks this
                                          (pronoun)
   past summer.

3. **A:** Why don't you **try on** the blue pants? They're very good-looking.

   B: I already _____ _____ _____ but I didn't like the
                                        (pronoun)
   way they fit.

4. **A:** Betty, please help Tommy **put on** his shoes.

   B: He _____ _____ _____ by himself.
                            (pronoun)

5. **A:** Who did Jan **go** shopping **with** this afternoon?

   B: I think she _____ _____ Annie.

6. **A:** Have the new fall sweaters **come in** yet?

    B: Yes. They _____ _____ last week.

7. **A:** You'd better **hang up** your raincoat so it'll dry out.

    B: I _____ _____ _____ as soon as I got here.
                               (pronoun)

8. **A:** What sizes did that shirt **come in**? Do you remember?

    B: If I remember correctly, it _____ _____ small, medium, and large.

9. **A:** I have to buy a blouse to **go with** those new slacks I bought last week.

    B: Why? The one you had on yesterday _____ very well _____

    _____ .
    (pronoun)

10. **A:** When are you going to **take back** those shoes that don't fit you?

    B: I _____ _____ _____ yesterday and got my
                                 (pronoun)
    money back.

Questions

1. What is the difference in meaning of the verb **go with** in Sentences 5 and 9?
2. What is the difference in meaning between **come ín** in Sentence 6 and **cóme in** in sentence 8? Can you think of other meanings of this verb?

Part II. Vocabulary Building

Following your instructor's directions, use ten of the words and expressions below and on the next page in dialogues or sentences of your own. Be sure that in the sentences or dialogues you write the meanings of the expressions you use will be clear to the reader.

get dressed up, be dressed up
  (choose one)
fashionable
for sale
on sale
kill time

waste time, a waste of time (choose one)
a becoming outfit, an attractive
     combination (choose one)
well-dressed, well-groomed (choose one)
alter, make alterations (choose one)
fit(s) well

window shopping
customer
match, go well together *(choose one)*
price tag

refund, credit voucher, receipt
  (choose one)
sales slip

NOTE: Of course, you may also use other vocabulary items from this lesson or from previous lessons.

LISTENING COMPREHENSION EXERCISE: STUDENT'S ANSWER SHEET

1. _____ **a)** getting undressed.

   _____ **b)** trying on new clothes.

   _____ **c)** getting dressed.

2. _____ **a)** You are wearing them.

   _____ **b)** You own them.

   _____ **c)** You need them.

3. _____ **a)** She's not going to buy the blouse.

   _____ **b)** It's not what she was looking for, but she'll buy it anyway.

   _____ **c)** She likes the blouse and she may buy it later.

4. _____ **a)** a man.

   _____ **b)** a woman.

   _____ **c)** either a man or a woman.

5. _____ **a)** I have something to do, but I'll do it later.

   _____ **b)** There is nothing special that I have to do.

   _____ **c)** I don't feel like buying anything.

6. _____ **a)** only to a man.

   _____ **b)** only to a woman.

   _____ **c)** to either a man or a woman.

7. _____ **a)** expensively dressed.

   _____ **b)** carefully dressed.

   _____ **c)** very fashionably dressed.

8. ____ **a)** wear any clothes.

____ **b)** wear elegant clothes.

____ **c)** wear his old clothes.

9. ____ **a)** have proof that I bought the item.

____ **b)** want a refund.

____ **c)** know the price of the item.

10. ____ **a)** being sold at a lower price than usual.

____ **b)** there for people to buy.

____ **c)** only there for people to look at.

CONVERSATION PRACTICE

Using words and expressions you have learned from the vocabulary used in the dialogues, choose one of the following situations and with a classmate make up a dialogue. Each person should speak at least three times: **A B, A B, A B** or **A B C, A B C, A B C.** Present it to the class according to your instructor's directions.

1. You have just bought a skirt or a pair of pants and you want a blouse or a shirt to go with the article of clothing. You ask a salesperson to show you something. He or she shows you several items and you ask for something less expensive. You finally find something you like.

2. You bought an article of clothing without trying it on. When you got home, you found that the garment didn't fit you well, and you didn't like the color after all. You take it back to the store and exchange it, or get a credit voucher, or ask for your money back.

3. You are looking for a certain article of clothing. (You decide which one.) The salesperson shows you several, but you don't see anything that you want to buy. You react accordingly.

4. You want to buy a new dress (or a suit) for a special occasion. (You choose the occasion.) You don't want to make a decision by yourself, so you ask someone to accompany you. (Use the two-word verb which means to accompany.)

5. You're looking for a certain item in a particular size and color. When you ask for it, the salesperson tells you that it is not available at the moment and suggests something similar. You like that item and decide to buy it.

146

6. A friend is wearing a good-looking outfit which you admire and which you think looks well on him or her. Make appropriate comments to your friend. Your friend responds accordingly.

7. Think of an experience you have had while shopping for clothes. Ask a classmate to work with you to make up a dialogue about that experience.

7. What does **do well** mean here?

8. How do you know **A** is working at the present time?

9. Has **A** been able to save any money from his present salary? How do you know? What's another way of saying "I'm always broke"?

6. **A:** Good morning. May I help you?

   B: Yes. I just received my **monthly statement**, and I can't make out the extra charges on it. I checked the back of the statement, but I still couldn't figure out what the charges were for.

   A: Could I please see your statement?

   B: Of course. Here it is.

   A: Which **item** isn't **clear** to you?

   B: Well, this one, NSF, and this other one, **overdraft** finance charge.

   A: Let's see. NSF simply means non-sufficient **funds**. You **made out** a check for $175, but you had only $171 in your account at that moment. So you were **overdrawn**. You tried to take more money out of the bank than you had funds. As you can see here, it also says "paid check charge." That means we paid the check, but we charged you a **fee** for paying it.

   B: Gee, I was positive I had enough in my account to **cover** that check, but sometimes I have trouble **balancing** my **checkbook**. At least the check didn't **bounce**.

   A: Sometimes it's just a mistake in arithmetic. When your bank statement arrives, **compare** it **with** your checkbook record. If you find a difference, **come back in.** I'll be glad to help you find the mistake.

   B: Thank you very much. You've been very helpful.

   A: Not at all. That's what we're here for.

Questions

1. What kind of information is included in a monthly bank statement?
2. What is the difference in meaning of the verb **make out** in the following two sentences? "I can't make out the extra charges." "You made out a check."
3. What do we mean when we say a check "bounces"?
4. According to **A**, what was the problem with **B**'s account?
5. What does the word **cover** mean here?
6. What kind of information does one usually have in a checkbook?
7. What does the expression to **balance (one's) checkbook** mean?
8. What's a synonym for **come back in** as the word is used here?

7. **A:** Excuse me, ma'am. How much is that pink silk dress in the window?

   B: It's $359.

A: Oh, my! That's way too much for my **budget**. Do you have anything similar to that but less expensive?

B: Well, we have this other style here for $150. It's very attractive.

A: H-m-m-m. That's still a little expensive for me, but I do like it. Do you have it in size 10?

B: Yes, we do. Would you like to try it on?

A: No, I'd better not. I might be tempted to buy it.

B: Do you have a **charge account** with us? Or a credit card?

A: No, I don't.

B: Well, if you're interested in the dress, we could put it on **layaway** for you. You can **put** a small amount **down** and then make some payment every week until it's paid for.

A: I'll have to **think** it **over**. I'd rather **save up for** it. I don't like to **buy** things **on time**.

B: It's a good buy. Well, if you decide to buy it, just ask for Gladys. I'll be glad to **wait on** you again.

Questions

1. What kind of a window is **A** referring to?

2. What's another way of saying "that's too much for my budget"?

3. Why doesn't **A** want to try on the other dress?

4. What is a charge account? How does it differ from a credit card?

5. What's another way of saying "you can put a small amount down"?

6. After reading this dialogue, can you explain what it means when you buy something on time?

8. **A:** What are you looking at in that magazine?

B: There's an **ad** for the most unusual chess set I've ever seen. I'd like to **send away for** it, but I can't **afford** it.

A: Let me see. Oh, that *is* beautiful but it *is* expensive. Maybe you could get it on an **installment plan**. Yes, it says here: "Send a personal check, a **money order**, or fill out the credit card information." It also says you can make a small **down payment** and then pay the rest in five monthly installments.

B: H-m-m-m. Maybe I can get it after all. It says they won't send the first **invoice** until after the first of the year. That's almost three months from now. I'll **send in** my order today. I'll use my Christmas bonus to pay the first installment.

A: Just make sure you don't **fall behind in** your payments or you'll **be up to your neck in debt**.

B: Don't worry. I'll make sure I budget for the payment every month till I get it paid off.

Questions

1. Why is **B** concerned about ordering the chess set?

2. According to the magazine advertisement, what are the four ways one can pay for the chess set?

3. Can you explain the difference between a layaway plan and an installment plan?

4. What are the various places one can buy a money order? Where do you usually buy one?

5. What is another word for **invoice**?

6. What time of the year does this conversation take place? How do you know?

7. How else can you say that someone is **in debt**?

8. What does it mean to be up to one's neck in debt?

9. What does **B** mean by "I'll budget for the payment"?

9. **A:** I just found a good part-time job. It's not much of a job, but I'll make enough to pay all my expenses.

B: My parents want me to concentrate on my studies so they're giving me an **allowance**.

A: An allowance? Aren't you lucky! Is it just for **spending money**?

B: No, it's to **cover all my expenses**. I go home the last weekend of the month and my father **writes out** a check for the next month's allowance.

A: What do you do—put the money in the bank until you need it?

B: Exactly. I cash my check and **divide** it **up**. I keep some for pocket money and deposit the rest in my **checking account**. I have to live on a strict budget. My parents think it's good training for me for later on when I'll **be on my own**— **supporting** myself.

Questions

1. What does **A** mean by "it's not much of a job"? What kind of work do you think the speaker might be doing?

2. Who are the speakers? How do you know?

3. Explain the meaning of the word **allowance** as it is used in this dialogue.

4. What's another way of saying "to cover one's expenses"? (See vocabulary, Dialogue 6.)

5. What's another way of saying "write out a check"? (See Dialogue 6.)

6. What does the expression **to be on one's own** mean?

7. What is meant by the term **spending money**? (In this dialogue, there's another expression that means the same thing. Can you find it?)

VOCABULARY

All of these words and expressions can be found in the dialogue for which they are listed. Although you may not have the occasion to use all of them, you should learn their meanings so that you will understand when you see them in print or when you hear another speaker use them.

DIALOGUE 1

moonlighting
make a (good) living
income
salary
lend
borrow
go along with
debts
ruin
pay off (S)

DIALOGUE 2

paycheck
credit card
pocket money
be short of cash
pay for
pay back (S)
help out (S)

DIALOGUE 3

payment
loan
penalty
branch
drive-in window
save time
cash a check
let (something) go by (S)
be due – payable as per schedule
stop off
take out (S) – withdraw
check on
bonus

DIALOGUE 4

savings account
deposit, deposit slip
withdrawal, withdrawal slip
interest rate
vary
transaction
form
passbook
open an account
make a deposit
settle for – accept

DIALOGUE 5

make – earn
take-home pay
raise – increase in salary
budget (v) – divide income to pay for
   one's expenses
make ends meet
do well
figure on – count on, expect
get by – manage, survive
be broke

DIALOGUE 6

monthly statement
item
funds
checkbook
clear
overdraft
overdraw
cover – pay for
bounce – be returned for insufficient funds
balance (v)
make out (S) – write
compare with (S)
come back in – re-enter

DIALOGUE 7

budget (n)
charge account
layaway (plan)
buy on time
put down (S) – make a partial payment
think over (S)
save up for
wait on

DIALOGUE 8

ad – advertisement
money order
invoice
down payment

installment plan
be up to (one's) neck in (something)
be in debt
send away for
send in (S)
fall behind in

DIALOGUE 9

allowance
spending money
cover (one's) expenses
checking account
support (oneself)
be on (one's) own
write out (S)
divide up (S)

QUESTIONS FOR CLASS DISCUSSION

NOTE TO THE INSTRUCTOR: We have tried to eliminate any questions which might cause a student embarrassment. Be sure to look over the exercise carefully before assigning it and eliminate any questions which you feel are inappropriate to the culture or situation in which the class is being given.

TO THE STUDENT: Answer these questions according to the directions given by your instructor.

1. Do you have or did you ever have a part-time or full-time job? What sort of work do you or did you do? What sort of deductions are or were taken out of your paycheck?

2. Have you ever moonlighted? What sort of work did you do?

3. Have you ever received a bonus of any sort?

4. Do you have an account at a bank? Which type of account?

5. If you have a checking account, have you ever had a problem balancing your checkbook?

6. What other services besides checking accounts and savings accounts do banks offer?

7. What are some of the reasons you might apply for a loan?

8. How do you feel about buying articles on time (using an installment plan)?

9. In your culture, is it a custom for parents to give sons and daughters an allowance? If so, at what age are children first given an allowance?

10. If you have credit cards, do you use them frequently? On what occasions or for what items do you prefer to pay cash?

11. Is the use of credit cards common in your culture?

12. If you live on a budget (that is, divide your income to cover your various expenses), do you usually manage to live within this budget? What sort of expenses might cause you to go over your budget?

13. Do you try to save a part of your income each week or month?

14. Is the habit of saving part of one's salary or income prevalent in your culture?

15. Have you ever bought an item you knew you couldn't afford? What were the circumstances that led you to buy that item?

16. How do you feel about borrowing money from friends or relatives?

17. How do you feel about lending money to friends or relatives? Have you ever had an unpleasant experience related to this practice?

18. In your culture, does one discuss private money matters with friends? How do you feel about this practice?

19. How often do you buy items because you like them and not because you need them?

20. When you go shopping for an expensive item, do you buy it immediately or do you shop around; that is, look at the item in various stores or shops and compare prices? Do you go home and think it over before making the purchase?

HOMEWORK

Part I. Incomplete Dialogues: Using Two-Word Verbs

These dialogues contain words or expressions similar to some of the two-word verbs contained in this lesson. From the list below, select the two-word verb which is closest in meaning to the boldface words in the statement and write it in the blanks. Use the past form of the verb whenever necessary. When you have completed the dialogues, read them aloud with another student. (Before you do the exercise, study the example.)

Example: **A:** Do you think Fred will **agree with** us on the project?
B: Oh, yes. I'm sure he'll __go__ __along__ __with__ us on that.

think over (S)	pay back (S)	put down (S)
go along with	come back in	take out (S)
figure on	send in (S)	make out (S)
get by	check on	compare with (S)

1. **A:** How much did you **write** that check for?

   B: I _____ it _____ for $50.00.

2. **A:** Did you **leave a deposit** for that dress you want to buy?

   B: I _____ $25.00 _____ . I'm buying it on layaway.

3. **A:** When will she **return** the money she borrowed from you?

   B: She'll _____ me _____ as soon as she gets her paycheck.

4. **A:** How soon after the fire drill did the children **re-enter** the classroom?

   B: They _____ _____ _____ after only five minutes.

5. **A:** Did you **expect** to get a bonus at the end of the year?

   B: We _____ _____ getting some kind of reward for all the hard work we did.

6. **A:** Sheila wants you to **get some information** about those new plastic containers.

   B: I've already _____ _____ them at the store.

7. **A:** How much money did you **withdraw** from the bank?

   B: I _____ _____ only a $100.00.

8. **A:** Is he going to **survive** on that low salary?

   B: I think so. He's been able to _____ _____ on it so far.

9. **A:** Did you **mail** the coupon for the free cookbook that was offered in that magazine?

   B: Yes, I _____ it _____ this morning.

10. **A:** Have you **considered** the job offer that Mr. Harrison made you?

    B: Yes, I've _____ it _____ carefully and I think I'm going to accept his offer.

Part II. Vocabulary Building

Following your instructor's directions, use the words and expressions that appear below in sentences or dialogues of your own. Be sure that the meaning of each word or expression is clear in the sentences or dialogues that you write. Use pronouns with the two-word verbs whenever appropriate.

installment plan, layaway
   (choose one)
budget (n *or* v)
checking account, savings account
   (choose one)
deposit (v), make a deposit
   (choose one)
withdraw, make a withdrawal
   (choose one)

make – earn
afford
fall behind (in)
help out (S)
pay off (S)
save up for
do well
pay for
let —— go by

> **NOTE:** Of course, you may also use other vocabulary items from this lesson or from previous lessons.

LISTENING COMPREHENSION EXERCISE: STUDENT'S ANSWER SHEET

1. ____ **a)** don't have to pay cash for it.

    ____ **b)** don't want to borrow money for it.

    ____ **c)** don't have the money for it.

2. ____ **a)** fasten my belt.

    ____ **b)** bring the two pieces together.

    ____ **c)** manage to live on my income.

3. ____ **a)** be paid more money for doing my job.

    ____ **b)** be starting a new job.

    ____ **c)** be awarded a prize for weight lifting.

4. ____ **a)** was made of rubber.

    ____ **b)** was returned for insufficient funds.

    ____ **c)** was stolen.

5. ____ **a)** be paid.

    ____ **b)** produce.

    ____ **c)** be able to save.

6. ____ **a)** took care of my business.

    ____ **b)** was expecting me.

    ____ **c)** asked me for a date.

7. ____ **a)** borrow some money.

    ____ **b)** put some money in the bank.

    ____ **c)** earn some money.

8. ____ **a)** some extra money.

____ **b)** some money owed to him.

____ **c)** an extra job.

9. ____ **a)** healthy.

____ **b)** successful.

____ **c)** happy.

10. ____ **a)** salary minus taxes and other deductions.

____ **b)** salary plus some extra money.

____ **c)** money I can earn at home.

CONVERSATION PRACTICE

Using words and expressions you have learned from the vocabulary lists or from the dialogues, choose one of the following situations and with a classmate make up a dialogue. Present it to the class according to your instructor's directions.

1. **At the Bookstore.** You (Student **A**) need a book for a particular class. You don't have enough money with you, but you must buy it right now because there is only one copy left. You ask a friend (Student **B**) to lend you a few dollars so that you can buy the book. Your friend agrees, and you arrange to pay back the money at a particular time.

2. **At the Bank.** You (Student **A**) want to open a checking account or a savings account. You ask a bank employee (Student **B**) about the minimum deposit required for the various accounts and decide which kind suits your needs. You also inquire about what other services the bank offers.

3. **At Home (on the telephone).** You (Student **A**) want to buy a radio that is being offered on sale in a newspaper advertisement. You call the store and ask the employee (Student **B**) about the different ways you can pay for the radio.

4. With another classmate, make up a dialogue similar to one in the lesson.

✈ 13

Let's Talk About Traveling

DIALOGUES

As you study these dialogues, pay particular attention to the boldface words and expressions. Some of them may already be in your vocabulary. You should be able to figure out the meanings of the others from the way in which they are used in the dialogues. When you have finished studying the dialogues, read them aloud with a friend or classmate. Be able to answer the questions at the end of each dialogue.

1. **A:** Excuse me, sir, could I please **check** your **boarding pass**? (Looking at the pass.) Uh, oh!

 B: Anything wrong?

 A: I think we've **run into** a problem here. I don't know how it happened, but we seem to have made duplicate seat assignments.

 B: Great! That's all I need.

 A: And I think this **flight** is **booked solid**.

 B: **Overbooked** perhaps? I just hope I'm not **bumped** and put on a later flight—I'll never make my appointment!

 A: What time did you **check in**?

 B: An hour ago. I **got off** a connecting flight from Miami in this same **terminal**, so I walked to this gate . . .

 A: (Looking at the boarding pass.) Oh, my gosh! You're on the wrong flight! This plane's going to San Diego.

 B: San Diego? Isn't this Flight 1142 to San José?

 A: Oh, no! You'd better **get off** this airplane fast. Ask our agent outside to help you out. Your flight probably hasn't **taken off** yet. Do you have any **luggage**?

 B: No. Thank God. I'm **traveling light**. I just have my **carry-on bag**.

 A: Boy! I don't believe this! This has been *some* day!

Questions

1. Where does this dialogue take place?
2. What seemed to be the problem at first? What was the real problem?
3. In which state of the United States are the cities of San Diego and San José located?
4. What was the passenger's reaction at first? Why do you think he reacted that way?
5. What's another way of saying "this flight is booked solid"? (There's another, similar expression in Dialogue 6.)
6. What does the expression **bumped** mean when applied to air travel?
7. What does the verb **check in** mean in reference to air travel? In other words, what exactly do passengers do when they check in?
8. If you were the passenger, what would you say to the agent outside the gate so that he or she could direct you to your flight as soon as possible?

9. What kind of day do you think **A** has had? Why do you think so?

10. What does the expression **travel light** mean?

At the Ticket Office in the Train Station

2. **A:** One **round trip** ticket to Washington, please.

B: **Express** or **local** train?

A: Express. Can I get anything to eat **on board**?

B: All our trains have a dining car with a snack bar. The next express leaves in ten minutes.

A: Will I be able to **make** it?

B: I'm sure you can, sir.

A: Why do you say that? Is it usually **delayed**?

B: Oh, no, sir. All our trains run on time. What I meant is that the train leaves from **track** one, right over there. See? Right across from this window. You can see the gate from here. The train is just **pulling in** now.

A: Yeah, I can see it. OK. How much do I owe you?

B: Fifty-three.

A: I'd better **get moving**. I don't want to **miss** that express.

B: Here's your ticket, sir. Track one. Oh, look. They've just turned the light on. Passengers can **board** now. The train won't **pull out** for at least eight minutes. You'll make it in plenty of time.

A: Thanks.

Questions

1. What's the difference in meaning between a **one-way ticket** and a **round-trip ticket**? Which kind of ticket to you think is usually more economical?

2. What's the difference between a local (regular) train and an express train?

3. What can you tell about the passenger from this dialogue?

4. How do you know **A** is a man?

5. What does **A** mean when he says he'd better get moving?

6. What other verbs could you use instead of **pull in** and **pull out**?

7. What does **make** mean in this dialogue?

3. **A:** Good evening, Miss. May I help you?

B: Good evening. I have a **reservation** for tonight. The name is Trent.

A: T-R-E-N-T? May I see your reservation number, please?

B: Sure. Here it is.

A: Thank you . . . (Looking at the computer screen.) Let's see . . . Trent, Mildred. You asked for a **double** . . . no, excuse me, a **single**—two nights. Right?

B: Right. Do you have any rooms available on one of the lower floors? I **have butterflies in my stomach** every time I think about a room on a high floor.

A: Is that so? Let me check them. All the rooms I have available are either on the eighth or the twenty-first floor.

B: I'll settle for the eighth floor.

A: Very well. Do you have your credit card?

B: Yes. You take Universal, don't you?

A: Yes, we do. Please fill out this **registration form**.

B: Certainly. (Fills it out.)

A: (After two or three minutes.) Here's your key.

B: (Surprised.) This is the key?

A: Yes. Actually, it's really a computerized card, but it works like a key. Just **insert** the card into the keyhole, and when the green light starts to flash, **push open** the door.

B: These modern devices people **come up with**!

A: Well, it's much safer this way. You see, with the card we can change the **combination** any time without having to change the lock. Anyway, I hope you enjoy your stay at the International.

B: Thanks. So do I. I've been looking forward to this trip for a long time. Oh, by the way, do I have to **check out** by noon?

A: Yes, but if you need to use the room for a couple of extra hours, we can make special arrangements. Please let the manager know **in advance**.

B: That's good to know. Thanks again.

A: You're welcome.

Questions

1. Where does this dialogue take place?
2. Why does **B** want a room on one of the lower floors?
3. What's the difference between a single and a double room? What other kinds of room arrangements would a large hotel have?
4. Why is **B** surprised when she gets the key to her room?
5. Is the International a large hotel? How can you tell?
6. What does **B** mean when she asks if she has to check out by noon? (The preposition **by** is the key word here.)
7. What do you think the special arrangements that **A** mentions could be?

4. **A:** May I help you?

B: We're interested in going on the **tour** to Green Island.

A: Half-day or all-day trip?

B: (Turning to friend.) What do you think?

C: (To **A**.) What's the difference in price?

A: The half-day trip is $25 and the all-day is $40.

B: That's not bad. (Turning to **C**.) What do you think? Should we take the all-day?

C: That's fine with me. Remember, I suggested that we **go Dutch,** but you insisted on **paying my way**. So I'm not going to complain.

B: (To **A**.) Do we have to bring our own food?

A: I'm afraid so. Check with the hotel. Some hotels provide **box lunches** for their guests. Or you could pick up a sandwich at the snack bar next door.

C: What about soda?

A: We do have beer and soda on board.

B: OK, then. **Book** us for tomorrow.

A: Name?

B: Wilkinson.

A: Wilkinson . . . party of two. We do require a **deposit** of fifty dollars.

B: Would a **traveler's check** be OK?

A: That's fine, ma'am. OK . . . here's your **receipt**. Be sure you bring it tomorrow morning. The boat **departs** at 8:00 sharp from that **pier** right over there. You can't **miss** it. Bring a hat and a shirt or jacket with long sleeves.

B: Thanks for the advice. (Aside to **C**.) I'm sure this is not a **tourist trap**.

Questions

1. What do you think is the relationship between **B** and **C**?
2. What does the expression **go Dutch** mean?
3. What does **B** mean by "book us"?
4. What kind of food would there be in a box lunch?
5. What's the difference in meaning between a **box lunch** and a **lunch box**?
6. What's the difference in meaning of the word **miss** in this dialogue and that verb in Dialogue 2?
7. Why do you think **A** told **B** and **C** to wear hats and long-sleeved shirts or jackets?
8. What does **B** mean by a **tourist trap**?

At the Ticket Window in a Bus Terminal

5. A: Good afternoon. Do you have a **bus schedule**?

B: Yes, ma'am. Here you are.

A: (After studying the schedule.) Are there any seats available on the 5:30 express bus to Burlington?

B: Sorry. It's **all booked**. That's the bus our regular **commuters** take, so it's usually **packed**. Besides, there's some sort of meeting in Burlington tonight.

A: That's why I'm going there. Is that the last bus of the day? I don't see any others listed.

B: We do have another one leaving at 6:30. It makes three stops, but it always arrives in Burlington **on schedule**. Are you interested?

A: No, I don't think so. It wouldn't get me there in time* for the meeting. I'll have to **skip it**. Thanks anyway.

B: You're welcome.

Questions

1. What does the expression **all booked** mean in this dialogue? (Find a synonym in Dialogue 1.)
2. Who is **B** referring to when he speaks of "our regular commuters"?
3. What's another way of saying "the bus is packed"?
4. Why didn't **A** take the other bus to Burlington?
5. What did **A** decide to do about the meeting?

6. A: You know, I must admit—I'm enjoying this **cruise** after all. I feel really relaxed.

B: You see? And you were so sure you'd be bored. I told you it would be a wonderful change for you.

A: Right. No meetings, nobody else's problems to solve. What's our next **port of call**, anyway? I haven't even checked the **itinerary**.

B: Lisbon. I've heard so much about the city. I'm looking forward to **sightseeing** and some shopping. I think we get there early in the morning.

A: Are you sure? Let me ask this gentleman. He must know. Excuse me, sir. What time do we arrive in Lisbon?

C: We're scheduled to **dock** at seven tomorrow morning.

A: Will we have the whole day **in port**?

C: Yes. The ship departs at midnight. You'll have plenty of time to shop and **tour** the city.

B: Do you know if we have to go through **immigration** and **customs**?

C: No, you don't. You get your **passports** back from the purser's office at the end of the cruise. Then you have to fill out a **declaration form**.

B: Thank you.

C: You're quite welcome. Enjoy your day **on shore**.

Questions

1. How are **A** and **B** traveling? How do you know?
2. How do you know that **A** wasn't enthusiastic about taking this trip at first?

---

* For an explanation of the use of the expression **in time** refer to Lesson 3, Dialogue 5.

3. What do you think **A**'s profession might be?

4. Who do you think **C** might be? Why do you think so? (Look at **A**'s third statement.)

5. How many hours will the ship be in Lisbon?

6. Where is Lisbon located?

7. Is Lisbon the last port of call? How can you tell?

7. **A:** Hey, Bill. I hear you and your wife are going away next month.

   B: Yeah. We decided it was about time to **take a trip**. We need a change—haven't had a real **vacation** in years.

   A: Where **are** you **headed**? Are you **going abroad**?

   B: We're going to Ireland. We got a terrific **package tour** on World Airways through a **travel agent**. By **making the reservations** well in advance we got a twenty-one day **excursion** at a very special **rate**. Everything's included—**air fare**, **ground transportation**, hotels, meals, **sightseeing tours**—everything.

   A: When are you leaving?

   B: Two weeks from tomorrow.

   A: That's super! All I can say is that I hope you have a good trip and enjoy every minute of it.

   B: Thanks, Hal. See you in about five or six weeks.

Questions

1. What do you think the relationship between **A** and **B** is? About how old do you think they might be?

2. Why are **B** and his wife taking a trip?

3. What does the expression **go abroad** mean?

4. What's another way of asking "where are you headed?"

5. What are some of the services a travel agent can provide?

6. Why does **B** think the package tour is terrific?

7. What is meant by the term **ground transportation**?

8. Explain what is meant by a **sightseeing tour**.

9. During what part of the month does this conversation take place? (Look at **A**'s first statement and **B**'s last statement.)

In the Baggage Claim Area of the Airport

8. **A:** That's funny. They seem to have finished **unloading** the **baggage** from our flight, and my **bag** hasn't come through yet. I wonder what's happened.

   B: Look! They've **turned off** the **baggage conveyor belt**. There's only one **suitcase** on it.

A: (Anxious.) And it's not mine! What do we do now? Maybe somebody **picked up** mine by mistake!

B: But they couldn't get out of here. They wouldn't have the right **baggage claim stub**. Let's ask the security guard what we should do.

A: Excuse me. My suitcase seems to have been lost—or stolen. Where do we go to report it?

C: Go to the Caribbean Airways baggage claim department office at the north end of this **concourse** and **file** a report.

A and B: Thanks very much.

At the baggage claim department office

D: Yes, may I help you?

A: I hope so. My suitcase is **missing**! We just came in on Flight 960 and all the baggage was **unloaded** and my suitcase didn't appear.

D: May I see your plane ticket, please? (Looking at the ticket.) It says you were a late check-in. You signed this yellow card saying you'd accept late **delivery** of your luggage.

A: I *do* remember signing something, but I was so **worried** that I wouldn't be able to **get on** the flight, I didn't even look at it. I got caught in a terrible **traffic jam** going to the airport and I boarded the plane at the last moment.

D: Then most probably your suitcase will arrive on the next flight from St. Thomas.

B: When's the next flight due?

D: Not until early tomorrow morning.

A and B: Tomorrow morning!

D: That's right. The office opens at 8:00. Bring your plane ticket with your baggage claim stub. Don't worry. I'm sure your suitcase will be waiting for you.

A and B: Thank you very much. Good night.

B: I sure hope he knows what he's **talking about**.

A: Me too. Boy, am I glad I **packed** my toothbrush and my makeup and a change of underwear in my carry-on bag!

B: Come on. Let's get a taxi to the hotel and get to bed. We'll have to be up very early tomorrow morning.

Questions

1. What do you think is the relationship between **A** and **B**?
2. Why did **B** think that **A**'s suitcase couldn't have been picked up by someone else?
3. What is a traffic jam? Why do you think it's called that? (Look up the meaning of the verb **jam**.)
4. What foolish thing did **A** do when she checked in at the airport in St. Thomas?
5. Where do you think St. Thomas is located?
6. What's the difference in meaning of the verb **pack** in this dialogue from that of the same verb in Dialogue 5?

VOCABULARY

All of the words and expressions listed below have been used in the dialogues of this lesson. Although you may not have the occasion to use all of them yourself, you should be able to understand them if you see them in print or hear another speaker using them.

DIALOGUE 1

check (v) – examine and verify
boarding pass
booked solid
overbook
flight
bump (off) – displace, remove from
terminal
luggage
travel light
carry-on bag
run into – confront
check in
get off – leave
take off – leave the ground in flight, depart

DIALOGUE 2

ticket office
train station
round-trip (ticket)
one-way (ticket)
local (train)
express (train)
board (v), on board
delay (v)
track
make – arrive in time
pull in, into
pull out (of)
miss - fail to get to a bus, plane, train in time

DIALOGUE 3

reservation
single (room)
double (room)

registration form
combination (lock)
insert (v)
have butterflies in (one's) stomach
push open (S)
come up with - invent, propose
check out
in advance

DIALOGUE 4

tour (n)
traveler's check
tourist trap
receipt
pier
go Dutch
pay (one's) way
book (v)
leave a deposit
miss – fail to see
depart

DIALOGUE 5

ticket window
bus schedule
all booked
commuter
packed – full, all seats occupied
on schedule
skip it

DIALOGUE 6

cruise
itinerary
port (of call), in port
sightseeing

dock (v)
tour (v)
immigration and customs
passport
declaration form
on shore

DIALOGUE 7

vacation
package tour
excursion
travel agent
rate
air fare
ground transportation
sightseeing tour
take a trip
make reservations
be headed
go abroad

DIALOGUE 8

baggage
baggage conveyor belt – carousel
baggage claim department office
baggage claim stub
suitcase – bag
concourse
delivery
traffic jam
missing – presumed lost
worried
unload
pack (v)
file (v)
get on
turn off (S)
pick up (S) – collect
talk about

QUESTIONS FOR CLASS DISCUSSION

> **NOTE TO THE INSTRUCTOR:** Choose the questions most appropriate to your particular teaching situation or for the amount of time you plan to devote to this activity.

1. Have you ever traveled outside the (your) country? To which country?

2. What are some of the most interesting places you've visited?

3. What's your favorite means of traveling? By plane, boat, or train?

4. What's the longest trip you've ever taken?

5. If you're on a pleasure trip, do you prefer to travel by yourself or with someone? Why?

6. For a short domestic trip would you rather travel by bus or train?

7. Have you ever run into a problem while on a trip? Explain.

8. Have you ever lost any luggage? If so, what were the results?

9. When you make reservations for a trip, do you do it through a travel agent or do you prefer to make the reservations with the airline yourself? Why or why not?

10. If you have traveled by plane, can you remember a particularly interesting flight or a frightening one?

11. What do you think of the food served on planes or trains? Do you remember any especially good or bad food you've been served?

12. Why do you think airlines overbook flights? Do you think this practice should be allowed? Why or why not?

13. Have you ever been bumped off a flight? Explain the circumstances. Do you think this practice should be allowed?

14. Have you ever missed a flight, a train or a bus? What was the reason? What was the consequence?

15. When you are traveling by yourself on a plane, a bus, or a train, do you ever engage in a conversation with the person or persons sitting near you? Explain.

16. If your answer to the previous question was yes, have you met any interesting people this way? Have you had any good or bad experiences as a result of it?

17. What do you usually do on a long trip by bus or train? Read? Sleep? Look out the window?

18. Have you ever been caught in a tourist trap? Describe what happened.

19. Do you know of any tourist traps in your city or country?

20. What has been your best or worst experience while traveling?

21. What items do you think people take in their carry-on luggage? What items would you carry?

22. During which season of the year would you prefer to travel? Why?

HOMEWORK

Part I. Incomplete Dialogues Using Two-Word Verbs

These dialogues contain some of the two-word verbs used in this lesson. Some of the verbs have irregular past-tense forms; others have regular -ed endings. Use pronouns in your answers, according to the object, and place these pronouns between the two parts of the separable two-word verbs.

   Example: Put on your shoes.   Put them on.

When you have completed the dialogues, practice reading them aloud with another student. Try to guess who the speakers might be in each of the dialogues.

1. **A:** Did Paul **run into** a problem with his reservation for Flight 846?

   B: Yes, he _____ _____ a big problem. His reservation hadn't been confirmed.

2. **A:** Did you **check in** at the registration counter?

    B: I _____ _____ as soon as we arrived at the hotel.

3. **A:** What time did you **check out** of the hotel?

    B: We _____ _____ before noon.

4. **A:** Were you able to **get on** that flight?

    B: Yes, I _____ _____ without any problem.

5. **A:** What time did Fred's plane **take off**?

    B: It _____ _____ ten minutes ago.

6. **A:** Tell Ben to **push** the door **open**.

    B: He's already _____ _____ _____ .
                                      (pronoun)

7. **A:** You'd better **pick up** your plane tickets from the travel agent.

    B: I _____ _____ _____ yesterday.
                              (pronoun)

8. **A:** When did your parents **go abroad**?

    B: They _____ _____ last summer.

9. **A:** Please **turn off** the radio.

    B: I just _____ _____ _____ .
                             (pronoun)

10. **A:** Have you ever **come up with** great ideas that haven't worked?

     B: I once _____ _____ _____ an idea that almost cost me my job.

Part II. Vocabulary Building

Following your instructor's directions, use the words and expressions that appear below in sentences or dialogues of your own. Be sure that the meaning of each word or expression is clear in the sentences or dialogues that you write.

round trip

excursion

sightseeing, sight-seeing tour
  (choose one)

traveler's check

reservation, make a reservation
  (choose one)

luggage, baggage (choose one)

delay (n or v) (choose one)

take a trip

booked solid, all booked (choose one)

travel light

go Dutch

be bumped (off)

check out (of), check in (choose one)

miss (a bus, train, plane)

get on, get off (choose one)

> **NOTE:** Of course, you may also use any other vocabulary items from this
> lesson or from any previous lesson.

LISTENING COMPREHENSION EXERCISE: STUDENT'S ANSWER SHEET

1. ____ **a)** enter the bus.

   ____ **b)** leave the bus.

   ____ **c)** stay on the bus.

2. ____ **a)** leave the train.

   ____ **b)** stay on the train.

   ____ **c)** enter the train.

3. ____ **a)** collect our luggage.

   ____ **b)** buy our luggage.

   ____ **c)** drop off our luggage.

4. ____ **a)** is going to leave the ground.

   ____ **b)** is going to fall to the ground.

   ____ **c)** is going to return to the terminal.

5. ____ **a)** solve a problem.

   ____ **b)** have a problem.

   ____ **c)** eliminate a problem.

6. ____ **a)** fail to make it.

   ____ **b)** fail to hit it.

   ____ **c)** fail to see it.

7. ____ **a)** You'll each pay for your own ticket.

   ____ **b)** You'll pay for your friend's ticket.

   ____ **c)** You'll use a credit card.

8. _____ **a)** was hit with something.

_____ **b)** was killed.

_____ **c)** was taken off the flight.

9. _____ **a)** have a stomachache.

_____ **b)** are nervous.

_____ **c)** are happy.

10. _____ **a)** pay the hotel.

_____ **b)** call the hotel.

_____ **c)** register at the hotel.

CONVERSATION PRACTICE

Using words and expressions you have learned from the vocabulary lists or from the dialogues, choose one of the following situations and with one or two classmates make up a dialogue in which each person speaks at least three times. Present it to the class according to your instructor's directions.

1. Go to a ticket window and ask for the train schedule to a particular city. Inquire about nonstop express service, food on board, and round-trip fare.

2. You arrive at a hotel late at night. You have no reservation, but you need a room. The hotel clerk informs you that the hotel is booked, but he or she also tells you that some guests have not arrived yet. Try to convince the clerk to give you a room.

3. You are sitting inside an airplane just before departure time. Another passenger comes over to you and tells you that you are sitting in his or her seat. You call the flight attendant, and he finds out you are on the wrong flight. You react accordingly and the flight attendant tells you what to do.

4. You and your friend would like to go on a special tour to Bird Island. Go to the tour desk at the hotel and inquire about the tour. Then decide whether or not you want to take the tour and, if so, how you will pay for it.

5. Make up a situation of your own similar to one of those in the dialogues of this lesson.

Review Lesson II

Choosing the Correct Verb: Using Two-Word Verbs

Here are several two-word verbs you have studied in Lessons 8 through 10. Most of those listed are appropriate to use in the dialogues which follow. Write the verbs which you think belong in the blank spaces in each of the dialogues. After you have completed the dialogues, read them aloud with a friend or a classmate.

have on	try on	take off
keep up with	puff up	take back
coming down with	put on	come back in
operated on	drop by	go with

1. **A:** Do you change your clothes when you get home from work?

   B: Of course. I _____ _____ my good clothes and _____ _____ something more comfortable—either jeans or shorts—depending on the weather.

2. **A:** Why don't you _____ _____ the new blue jeans your mother bought for you?

   B: I already did. They're too small. I'll have to _____ them _____ and exchange them for a larger size.

3. **A:** What's the matter with you? Your eyes are all red and swollen. You look as if you're _____ _____ _____ the flu or something.

   B: No. It's just an allergy. I ate tomatoes and I shouldn't have. I always have an allergic reaction which makes my eyes _____ _____ .

4. **A:** I heard your grandmother fell and broke her hip. Is she still in the hospital?

   B: Yes. She was _____ _____ last week and she's doing fine. Why don't you _____ _____ during visiting hours? I know she'd love to see you.

> **NOTE:** The verbs below are for the next five sentences.

feel up to	take off	warm up
cut down on	help out	write out
fall behind in	figure on	take out
put on	drive out	go out

1. **A:** Would you like to _____ _____ to that new restaurant on Route 3? It's a nice day for a ride.

   B: I don't think so. I'm kind of tired. I'll just _____ _____ some leftovers in the microwave. We can _____ _____ for dinner during the weekend.

2. **A:** Why don't you _____ _____ a check for this month's installment on the car right now so you don't forget it?

   B: That's a good idea. I don't want to _____ _____ _____ the payments. It wouldn't be good for my credit rating.

3. **A:** How much money are you planning to _____ _____ of your savings account to do your Christmas shopping?

   B: Five hundred dollars, I guess. I _____ _____ spending about that much altogether.

4. **A:** Why are you on a diet again? You don't need to _____ _____ any more weight.

   B: Oh, yes I do. I _____ _____ five pounds over the holidays.

5. **A:** I have so much housecleaning to do and I just don't _____ _____ _____ doing it. I'm still not completely over my cold.

   B: Don't worry. I'll be glad to _____ you _____ . If we work together we can finish it in no time.

VOCABULARY BUILDING

Part I. Choosing the Correct Word: Lessons 8–10

On page 180 are several vocabulary items you have studied in Lessons 8 through 10. Complete the following dialogues by writing the correct words or expressions in the blanks. *Be sure to use the correct tenses and forms of the verbs.* After you have completed the dialogues, practice reading them aloud with a friend or classmate.

epidemic	brunch	checkup	stuffed up
meals	contagious	come down with	take a pill
prescription	catch	keep up with	out of shape
snack	appetite	be out	be exposed to

1. **A:** We usually eat only two _____ on Sunday, breakfast and dinner.

   B: We do too, except we have a _____ about eleven o'clock

   because everybody sleeps late. Then we eat an early dinner.

2. **A:** Did your doctor give you a _____ for your bronchitis?

   B: Yes, I have to _____ _____ _____ three times a day

   for ten days and then go in for a _____ .

3. **A:** Don't walk so fast. I can't _____ _____ _____ you.

   B: You're _____ _____ _____ because you haven't

   been getting enough exercise.

4. **A:** You're not eating your dinner. Are you _____ _____

   _____ the flu?

   B: No, I had a _____ at four o'clock—some potato chips and

   a soda. Now I don't have any _____ .

5. **A:** My nose is all _____ _____ . I think I'm

   _____ a cold.

   B: I'm not surprised. When you work in an office with so many people you can't

   help but _____ _____ _____ colds.

6. **A:** There's an _____ of chickenpox in the elementary school.

   Thirty children _____ _____ sick.

   B: Chickenpox is a very _____ disease, isn't it?

Part II. Choosing the Correct Word: Lessons 11–13

You studied the following vocabulary in Lessons 11 through 13. Complete the dialogues by writing the correct word or expression in the blanks. *Be sure to use the correct tenses and forms of the verbs.* After you have completed the dialogues, practice reading them aloud with a friend or classmate.

deposit	receipt	on sale	get dressed
paycheck	take-home pay	get going	make a living
sales slip	refund	in ages	make it
reservation	deductions	go with	have on
salary			

1. A: I'd like to make a _____ for two for the Historic

Monument Tour tomorrow morning. Do I have to leave a _____ ?

    B: Yes, sir. Ten dollars. Please write your name and room number right here.

(After a minute or two.) Thank you. Here's your _____ .

You pay the rest of the money tomorrow morning before the tour begins.

2. A: You'd better hurry up and _____ _____ . The plane

leaves at three.

    B: I know. I'm all ready except for my shoes and my jewelry. If we don't _____

_____ , we'll never _____ _____ .

3. A: Chris, I haven't seen you _____ _____ ! Where have you been?

    B: Right here—working hard to _____ ____ _____

like everybody else. I guess we just have different schedules.

4. A: I'm going to return these shoes I bought _____ _____ . They

don't fit me very well. I should have tried them on.

    B: You'll need your _____ _____ if you expect them

to give you a _____ .

5. **A:** Bill's _____ has gone up considerably. He's making a lot more money than he was a few years ago.

B: But his _____ _____ _____ isn't that much more. He has so many _____ from his _____ .

6. **A:** What a beautiful necklace you _____ _____ ! The beads are almost exactly the same color as the flowers in your dress.

B: Thank you. I was lucky to find something to _____ _____ this dress. The flowers are such an unusual shade of blue.

Part III. Homework Exercise: Writing Sentences

Many two-word verbs have more than one meaning. All of the verbs listed below have been used in Lessons 8 through 13, and all of them have been used with two or three different meanings. Write sentences or dialogues of your own using each of these items. The meanings of the verbs are given in parentheses after the verbs.

come in (arrive)
cóme in* (obtainable, available)
come ín (enter)
go with (match)
go with (accompany)
take off (remove)
take off [pounds] (lose weight)

take off (leave the ground)
wear out (use until the item is useless)
wear out (*usually past tense:* tired)
pass out** (distribute)
pass out (lose consciousness)
get off (finish work)
get off (leave a bus, plane, train)

_____

* **Cóme in**, meaning *obtainable* or *available*, is pronounced with the stress on the first word.

** This verb appears in Lesson 2.

1. ____ **a)** lost consciousness.

   ____ **b)** left the tennis court.

   ____ **c)** hit the ball too hard.

2. ____ **a)** become unusable.

   ____ **b)** be wearable outside.

   ____ **c)** go out of style.

3. ____ **a)** food someone else threw out.

   ____ **b)** food that was overcooked.

   ____ **c)** food remaining from a previous meal.

4. ____ **a)** a book of coupons for free admission to a sports event.

   ____ **b)** a record of a savings account.

   ____ **c)** a document required for international travel.

5. ____ **a)** continues as he is doing.

   ____ **b)** tries to get even better grades.

   ____ **c)** saves all his report cards.

6. ____ **a)** buying new windows for our house.

   ____ **b)** looking at merchandise on display in store windows.

   ____ **c)** buying something displayed in a store window.

7. ____ **a)** bought.

   ____ **b)** borrowed.

   ____ **c)** wore.

8. _____ **a)** recovering from.

_____ **b)** preparing for.

_____ **c)** going through.

9. _____ **a)** a list of ingredients for the stew.

_____ **b)** the cost of making the stew.

_____ **c)** the name of the stew.

10. _____ **a)** carry only a little baggage.

_____ **b)** travel during the daylight hours.

_____ **c)** carry light-colored suitcases.

11. _____ **a)** student group.

_____ **b)** cruise.

_____ **c)** pleasure trip.

12. _____ **a)** fresh.

_____ **b)** not fatty.

_____ **c)** well-cooked.

13. _____ **a)** cure.

_____ **b)** reason.

_____ **c)** doctor.

14. _____ **a)** receipt.

_____ **b)** check.

_____ **c)** bill.

15. _____ **a)** slim.

_____ **b)** young.

_____ **c)** tall.

Scripts for Listening Comprehension Exercises

LESSON 1

Listen to each dialogue carefully. Then listen to the questions and put a check mark next to the sentence which you think is the best answer. Check only one.

Let's practice with this dialogue:

A: I'm having a lunch in honor of Kathy's birthday next Saturday. I hope you can make it.

B: I'm terribly sorry. I won't be able to. I have to work that day.

"I hope you can make it" means:

_____ **a)** I'd like you to prepare the lunch.

_____ **b)** I'd like you to bring a present.

__✔__ **c)** I'd like you to come.

The correct answer is **c)**. Now let's begin.

1. **A:** Professor Johnson, may I present my mother, Dr. Wilson? Mother, this is my English professor, Dr. Mary Johnson.

  B: How do you do, Dr. Wilson. It's a pleasure to meet you.

  A: How do you do, Dr. Johnson. The pleasure is mine.

The people in this dialogue are using the expression **How do you do?** because:

_____ **a)** It is an informal way of saying hello.

_____ **b)** They are being introduced to each other.

_____ **c)** One person is asking the other how she feels.

2. **A:** (Sound of telephone ringing.) Hello.

  B: Hi, darling. I'm leaving the office now. Do you need anything from the supermarket?

  A: Well, you can pick up some ice cream. We don't have anything for dessert.

  B: OK. I'll be home in about half an hour.

In this dialogue, the verb **pick up** means:

     ____ **a)** collect.

     ____ **b)** look for.

     ____ **c)** buy.

3. **A:** How many people were there at the meeting?

     B: Quite a few. I saw several people I didn't know.

In this dialogue the expression **quite a few** means:

     ____ **a)** a rather large number.

     ____ **b)** not very many.

     ____ **c)** almost none.

4. **A:** Hi, Jill. How're you doing?

     B: Fine, thanks. And you?

     A: Just fine. I'm on my way to get a cup of coffee. Why don't you come along?

     B: Sorry, Ruth. I have a class now and I'm already late. I'll take a rain check, though. So long.

     A: OK. See you later.

"I'll take a rain check" means:

     ____ **a)** I can't. I have to cash a check.

     ____ **b)** I'll go if it doesn't rain.

     ____ **c)** I can't go now, but I'd like to go some other time.

5. **A:** How's the project coming along?

     B: Great! I'll be able to finish it this afternoon. I'm looking forward to going home for the weekend.

In this dialogue, **looking forward to** means:

     ____ **a)** I'll be able to go home.

     ____ **b)** I want very much to go home.

     ____ **c)** I have to go home.

6. **A:** It's good to see you after such a long time. When can we get together?

B: I'll call you next week. We can make a date for lunch.

A: Great! I'll be expecting your call.

In this dialogue, **make a date** means:

_____ **a)** We'll look at the calendar.

_____ **b)** We'll arrange to meet.

_____ **c)** We'll prepare lunch.

7. **A:** I heard you rode in the bike race yesterday. How was it?

B: Great! I didn't win anything, but I had a wonderful time. I ran into some friends I hadn't seen for a long time.

In this dialogue, **ran into** means:

_____ **a)** I hit them with the bike.

_____ **b)** I met them by chance.

_____ **c)** I arranged to meet them.

8. **A:** Hi, how're you doing?

B: Pretty well, thanks. I'm beginning to learn my way around the campus.

A: It's quite a big place, isn't it?

B: It certainly is. At the college I came from the campus was very small.

In this dialogue, the word **campus** means:

_____ **a)** a field or open space outside of a city.

_____ **b)** the grounds of a university or college.

_____ **c)** a place to go camping.

9. **A:** Your first name is very unusual, isn't it?

B: I've never thought about it, but I guess it is. It was my mother's maiden name.

A maiden name is:

_____ **a)** a word referring to an unmarried woman.

_____ **b)** a woman's name before she is married.

_____ **c)** a nickname.

10. **A:** Do you know Tom Blake?

B: Of course I do. Tom and I are colleagues at the university.

In this dialogue the word **colleague** means:

_____ **a)** We're both members of the same sports organization.

_____ **b)** We're both students at the university.

_____ **c)** We both teach at the university.

LESSON 2

I'm going to read parts of sentences. You are to choose the expression which you think best finishes each sentence. Put a check on the line to the left of the expression you choose. Mark only one for each sentence. I'll read each sentence twice.

1. When I cross out a word I:

_____ **a)** draw a line under it.

_____ **b)** draw a line around it.

_____ **c)** draw a line through it.

2. When Professor Larkin calls on Joseph, she is asking him to:

_____ **a)** answer a question orally.

_____ **b)** write in his notebook.

_____ **c)** speak on the telephone.

3. When Janet says she wants to copy over her assignment, she means she wants to:

_____ **a)** write it again on another piece of paper.

_____ **b)** make changes in what she has written.

_____ **c)** look at another student's assignment.

4. When Professor White asks Maritza to do her homework over, he wants her to:

_____ **a)** do it again correctly.

_____ **b)** make an exact copy.

_____ **c)** write on the other side of the paper.

5. When Roberto says he is going to look over his notes to prepare for a quiz, he's going to:

_____ **a)** use a dictionary.

_____ **b)** review what he has written.

_____ **c)** get more information.

6. When I underline a word I:

_____ **a)** draw a line through it.

_____ **b)** draw a line around it.

_____ **c)** draw a line under it.

7. When Mr. Bower says he's going to call the roll he is going to:

_____ **a)** ask for some bread.

_____ **b)** take attendance.

_____ **c)** act in a play.

8. When Mary says she used to collect dolls she means she:

_____ **a)** still collects them.

_____ **b)** collected them in the past but not now.

_____ **c)** is accustomed to collecting them.

9. When Mrs. Jones says, "John, please pay attention in class," she is asking him to:

_____ **a)** listen carefully.

_____ **b)** attend the class.

_____ **c)** give some money.

10. When Jack says, "At first I didn't want to get up early but now I'm getting used to it," he means:

_____ **a)** He likes getting up early now.

_____ **b)** He doesn't get up early anymore.

_____ **c)** He's accustomed to getting up early now.

LESSON 3

Part I

In your textbook you will see five clocks each with only the hours (numbers) shown on them. As I read the time for each clock, draw in the hands in the correct position. Ready? I'll say each time twice. Be sure to draw the minute hand longer than the hour hand.

1. It's a quarter after six.
2. It's half-past three.
3. It's ten minutes before one.
4. It's a quarter to eight.
5. It's 2:20.

Part II

I'm going to read parts of sentences. You are to choose the expression which you think best finishes each sentence. Put a check on the line to the left of the expression you choose. Mark only one for each sentence. I'll read each sentence twice.

1. When Alec said he just glanced at the notice on the blackboard, he meant:

_____ **a)** He looked at it quickly.

_____ **b)** He looked at it carefully.

_____ **c)** He looked at it for a long time.

2. If Alan says he overslept yesterday morning, he means:

_____ **a)** He slept at a friend's house.

_____ **b)** He slept longer than he had planned to sleep.

_____ **c)** He slept badly.

3. When Maria asks her friend if she will stay with the children tonight, she wants her friend to:

_____ **a)** take care of the children.

_____ **b)** take the children to her house.

_____ **c)** visit the children.

4. If I say that the alarm goes off at six o'clock every morning I mean that:

_____ **a)** It rings or makes a loud sound.

_____ **b)** It explodes.

_____ **c)** It stops functioning.

5. When Frederick says he's going to take a nap, he means:

_____ **a)** He's going to sleep for a short time.

_____ **b)** He's going to eat something.

_____ **c)** He's going for a walk.

LESSON 4

Part I

I'm going to read parts of sentences. You are to choose the expression which you think best finishes the sentence. Put a check on the line to the left of the expression you choose. Mark only one for each sentence. I'll read each sentence twice.

1. If I ask you to jot down some information, I want you to:

_____ **a)** listen to it.

_____ **b)** write it.

_____ **c)** look for it.

2. When Peter says he has to brush up on his lecture notes, he means he's going to:

_____ **a)** review them.

_____ **b)** write them again.

_____ **c)** look for them.

3. When Ana says she's due at the library at two, she means she:

_____ **a)** wants to be there.

_____ **b)** is scheduled to be there.

_____ **c)** can be there.

4. If Henry tells you he talked over his plans with his father, he means they:

_____ **a)** discussed his plans.

_____ **b)** disagreed about his plans.

_____ **c)** decided on his plans.

5. If I tell you I cut class today, I mean:

_____ **a)** I went to class.

_____ **b)** I taught class.

_____ **c)** I was absent from class.

Part II

Now you're going to hear some dialogues using some two-word verbs from this lesson. On your paper you will find three parts of sentences next to each number. Put a check next to the one which best explains the meaning of the verb in the dialogue.

1. A: Your blue suit needs to be cleaned.
   B: I know. I dropped it off at the laundry on my way home.

"I dropped it off" means I:

_____ **a)** let the suit fall to the floor.

_____ **b)** left it.

_____ **c)** picked it up.

2. A: What are you doing right now?
   B: I'm taking down some information from the textbook.

"I'm taking down some information" means I'm:

_____ **a)** removing it.

_____ **b)** writing it.

_____ **c)** reading it.

3. A: What's the matter? Why are you so upset?
   B: When I typed the letter, I left out a sentence.

"I left out a sentence" means I:

_____ **a)** added a sentence.

_____ **b)** underlined a sentence.

_____ **c)** omitted a sentence.

4. **A:** Where are you going?

B: To the library to take out a book for my history assignment.

In this dialogue "to take out a book" means to:

_____ **a)** borrow a book.

_____ **b)** return a book.

_____ **c)** buy a book.

5. **A:** Did you do the last question on the test?

B: No. I couldn't figure it out.

"I couldn't figure it out" means that I couldn't:

_____ **a)** do the arithmetic for it.

_____ **b)** remember the answer to it.

_____ **c)** understand it.

LESSON 5

We're going to read some dialogues using some of the expressions you have studied in this lesson. In your textbook there are three possible answers for each question. Put a check beside the letter of the answer you think is the best.

1. **A:** Have you seen Tom lately?

B: Yes, as a matter of fact he came by my house last night.

In this dialogue, **came by** means:

_____ **a)** stayed.

_____ **b)** visited.

_____ **c)** bought.

2. A: Who do you think Jill resembles most?

   B: I think she takes after her father a lot.

In this dialogue, **takes after** means:

_____ **a)** follows.

_____ **b)** goes ahead of.

_____ **c)** looks like.

3. A: Why did you and Tom move to this community?

   B: Because we thought it would be a good place to bring up a family.

In this dialogue, the verb **bring up** means:

_____ **a)** leave.

_____ **b)** raise.

_____ **c)** take.

4. A: Where are the children this afternoon?

   B: With my next-door neighbor. She's looking after them.

In this dialogue, **looking after** means:

_____ **a)** taking care of.

_____ **b)** looking for.

_____ **c)** calling for.

5. A: Did you hear the wonderful news about Pat and Jeff?

   B: Yes. It's incredible. I still can't get over it.

In this dialogue, **get over** means:

_____ **a)** recover from it.

_____ **b)** believe it.

_____ **c)** forget it.

6. A: How did you make out on the history test?

   B: I got the answers to two questions mixed up.

In this dialogue, "I got the answers mixed up" means:

_____ **a)** I confused one answer with the other.

_____ **b)** I left out two questions.

_____ **c)** I answered the questions correctly.

7. A: Where are you going this summer?

   B: I'm going to visit my folks in the country for a while.

In this dialogue, **my folks** refers to my:

_____ **a)** friends.

_____ **b)** grandparents.

_____ **c)** parents.

8. A: Did you know that my kid brothers are twins? Here's a photo of them.

   B: No. I didn't. Heavens! They're identical. How can you tell them apart?

In this dialogue, the verb **tell apart** means:

_____ **a)** say something to them.

_____ **b)** leave them alone.

_____ **c)** distinguish one from the other.

9. A: How is your grandfather doing?

   B: He's elderly, but he's healthy and active.

In this dialogue, **elderly** means:

_____ **a)** troublesome.

_____ **b)** old.

_____ **c)** sick.

10. A: What are you doing this holiday weekend?

   B: I'm planning to go away for a few days:

In this dialogue, the verb **go away** means:

_____ **a)** stay around.

_____ **b)** make a date.

_____ **c)** take a short trip.

LESSON 6

Part I

You're going to hear some dialogues using two-word verbs you have studied in this lesson. On your answer sheet you will find three expressions next to each number. Put a check on the line to the left of the expression you think best explains the meaning of the two-word verb used in the dialogue. Each dialogue will be read twice.

1. **A:** Are you and Tina going out tonight?

B: Yes, we are. We're planning to take in a movie with another couple.

In this dialogue, the verb **take in** means:

_____ **a)** We're going to see a movie in a theater.

_____ **b)** We're going to watch a TV movie.

_____ **c)** We're going to use a movie camera.

2. **A:** Can you come over for dinner on Saturday?

B: I'd love to. I don't have anything on for this weekend.

In this dialogue, the verb **have on** means:

_____ **a)** I'm not wearing any clothes.

_____ **b)** I don't have any other plans.

_____ **c)** I don't have anything more important to do.

3. **A:** What're we going to have for dinner? There's not much food in the refrigerator.

B: Don't worry. I'm sure Chris will whip up something good for us.

In this dialogue, the verb **whip up** means:

_____ **a)** Chris will buy some food on the way home from work.

_____ **b)** Chris will prepare something quickly.

_____ **c)** Chris will ask a friend to bring something for dinner.

4. **A:** What time is Maria expecting us for dinner?

B: About 7:00. I'll pick you up at 6:30.

In this dialogue, the verb **pick up** means:

_____ **a)** I'll get in touch with you.

_____ **b)** I'll call you up.

_____ **c)** I'll come to get you.

5. **A:** How are you and Tony going to celebrate your birthday?

 B: We're going to have some friends over on Saturday night.

In this dialogue, the verb **have over** means we're going to:

_____ **a)** visit some friends.

_____ **b)** invite some friends to our house.

_____ **c)** go out with some friends.

Part II

Now we will read dialogues using some of the expressions you have studied in this lesson. In your textbook there are three possible answers for each question. Put a check on the line next to the correct answer.

1. **A:** Are you and Tom going to the dance?

 B: Yes we are. We have a double date with Sarah and Pete.

In this dialogue the expression: **double date** means:

_____ **a)** two pieces of fruit.

_____ **b)** two calendar days.

_____ **c)** a social engagement with another couple.

2. **A:** Could you please give me a hand with this? It's very heavy.

 B: Certainly. I'll be glad to.

In this dialogue, "Please give me a hand with this" means:

_____ **a)** Please shake hands with me.

_____ **b)** Please help me.

_____ **c)** Please let me take your hand.

3. **A:** You and your friend seem to have a lot of fun.

 B: Yes, we do. We have a lot of things in common.

In this dialogue, "We have a lot of things in common" means:

    ____ **a)** We like very ordinary things.

    ____ **b)** We are interested in the same things.

    ____ **c)** We both have the same things.

4. **A:** How are you going to celebrate your anniversary?

    B: We're going to have an open house.

In this dialogue, "an open house" refers to:

    ____ **a)** a building with many windows.

    ____ **b)** a house with a big open terrace.

    ____ **c)** a kind of party.

5. **A:** What do you have in mind for Saturday night?

    B: Nothing special.

In this dialogue, "What do you have in mind?" means:

    ____ **a)** What are you planning?

    ____ **b)** What are you cooking?

    ____ **c)** What are you imagining?

REVIEW LESSON I

We are going to read some dialogues using vocabulary items, including two-word verbs, from the lessons you have studied so far. On your answer sheet you will find three possible answers to each question. Put a check next to the letter of the answer you think is correct.

1. **A:** Did you speak to your history professor about your term paper?

    B: Yes, I did. We talked over some of the problems I'm having with it.

In this dialogue, the verb **talked over** means:

    ____ **a)** repeated.

    ____ **b)** discussed.

    ____ **c)** solved.

2. **A:** Did you get that address? I'll repeat it for you.

      B: Just a minute. I want to jot it down.

In this dialogue, the verb **jot down** means:

    ____ **a)** write.

    ____ **b)** investigate.

    ____ **c)** find.

3. **A:** Are you going to hand in your report today?

      B: No, I'm not. I have to copy it over first.

In this dialogue, the verb **copy over** means:

    ____ **a)** write on the other side of the paper.

    ____ **b)** write it again in its present form.

    ____ **c)** revise it completely.

4. **A:** How are the students going to pay for the graduation party?

      B: They're going to ask everyone to chip in for it.

In this dialogue, the verb chip in means:

    ____ **a)** make a suggestion.

    ____ **b)** bring a friend.

    ____ **c)** contribute some money.

5. **A:** What's the assignment for tomorrow? I didn't hear it.

      B: I'm sorry. I didn't hear it either. I dozed off for a few minutes.

In this dialogue, the verb dozed off means:

    ____ **a)** I didn't pay attention.

    ____ **b)** I fell asleep.

    ____ **c)** I left the room.

6. **A:** I'm sorry, Professor. I didn't hear the instructions.

      B: I said, "Cross out the first three words on line three."

In this dialogue, the verb **cross out** means:

_____ **a)** put a mark next to the verbs.

_____ **b)** erase the words.

_____ **c)** draw a line through the words.

7. **A:** What did the professor ask us to do? I couldn't hear her.

   B: She asked us to underline the verbs in the sentences.

In this dialogue, the verb **underline** means:

_____ **a)** draw a line through the verbs.

_____ **b)** put accent marks on the verbs.

_____ **c)** draw a line beneath the verbs.

8. **A:** Are you going to work during the summer?

   B: Of course. I have to earn money for my tuition next fall.

In this dialogue, the word **tuition** means:

_____ **a)** money to pay for my courses.

_____ **b)** money to pay for my food.

_____ **c)** money to pay the rent.

9. **A:** Have you been studying long?

   B: Too long. I'm so drowsy I can hardly keep my eyes open.

In this dialogue, the word **drowsy** means:

_____ **a)** sleepy.

_____ **b)** sick.

_____ **c)** bored.

10. **A:** Do you have to get up at five o'clock tomorrow morning? That's awfully early.

   B: That's OK. I'll take a nap in the afternoon.

In this dialogue, the expression **take a nap** means:

_____ **a)** I'll sleep for a short time.

_____ **b)** I'll have a snack.

_____ **c)** I'll go for a walk.

11. **A:** Do you know what I'm talking about?

   B: Yes. I've got it straight now.

In this dialogue, the expression I've **got it straight** means:

   _____ **a)** I've heard of it.

   _____ **b)** I understand it.

   _____ **c)** I'll figure it out later.

12. **A:** Professor, do you have any appointments this afternoon?

   B: Well, I'm having lunch with a colleague at one o'clock.

In this dialogue, the word **colleague** means:

   _____ **a)** a close relative.

   _____ **b)** a former student.

   _____ **c)** another professor.

13. **A:** Do you know that man? You keep looking at him.

   B: He looks very familiar to me.

In this dialogue, the expression **looks very familiar** means:

   _____ **a)** He resembles a member of my family.

   _____ **b)** I think I've seen him before.

   _____ **c)** I think he's a distant relative.

14. **A:** What time did you get up this morning?

   B: I set the alarm to go off at six, but I didn't get up till seven.

In this dialogue, the expression to **set the alarm** means:

   _____ **a)** I turned on the alarm at six.

   _____ **b)** I turned off the alarm at six.

   _____ **c)** I wanted the alarm to ring at six.

15. **A:** Did you enjoy your vacation?

   B: It was a wonderful change from my usual daily routine.

In this dialogue, the word **routine** means:

_____ **a)** schedule.

_____ **b)** responsibilities.

_____ **c)** problems.

LESSON 8

The sentences you are going to hear contain some of the words and expressions you have studied in this lesson. I'll read each sentence twice. Just listen the first time. When I read the sentence the second time, put a check on the line to the left of the sentence or phrase which gives the best meaning for the word or expression used in the sentence.

1. If Gary says he will take care of the food for the party he means he will:

_____ **a)** provide it.

_____ **b)** taste it.

_____ **c)** watch it.

2. When a recipe calls for lean meat, it refers to meat that:

_____ **a)** contains little fat.

_____ **b)** is well cut.

_____ **c)** is clean.

3. If a friend says that she is going to have a snack, she means that she is going to eat:

_____ **a)** lunch.

_____ **b)** a light meal.

_____ **c)** a heavy meal.

4. Ground meat refers to meat that has been:

_____ **a)** crushed into fine particles.

_____ **b)** cut into pieces.

_____ **c)** thrown to the ground.

5. If I invite some friends for brunch, I will expect them to arrive:

    ____ **a)** around eleven in the morning.

    ____ **b)** at noon or later.

    ____ **c)** early in the morning.

6. If you ask about the seasoning for a particular food, you want information concerning:

    ____ **a)** what spices or condiments to use.

    ____ **b)** the time of year when it is served.

    ____ **c)** the cooking method used.

7. When you say you don't care for any coffee right now, you mean:

    ____ **a)** You don't like it.

    ____ **b)** It makes no difference one way or the other.

    ____ **c)** You don't want any.

8. When a menu offers chicken stew, it refers to:

    ____ **a)** fried chicken.

    ____ **b)** chicken cut up and broiled.

    ____ **c)** chicken boiled in a sauce.

9. When I tell you that I'll give you a buzz, I mean that:

    ____ **a)** I'll make a noise.

    ____ **b)** I'll call you by telephone.

    ____ **c)** I'll hit you.

10. If I say that my day off is all taken up, I mean that:

    ____ **a)** I'll take off on a trip.

    ____ **b)** I'll have nothing to do.

    ____ **c)** I'll be busy all day.

LESSON 9

The sentences you are going to hear contain some of the expressions you have studied in this lesson. I'll read each sentence twice. Just listen the first time. When I read the sentence the second time, put a check on the line to the left of the sentence or phrase which is the best meaning of the expression used in the sentence.

1. When a man says that he is in shape, he means that he:

_____ **a)** has a particular body build.

_____ **b)** is below normal weight.

_____ **c)** is in good physical condition.

2. A person who is out of breath needs to:

_____ **a)** go to an air-conditioned room.

_____ **b)** rest a few minutes.

_____ **c)** drink something cold.

3. If Jaime says he wasn't cut out for hockey, he means he:

_____ **a)** didn't like the game.

_____ **b)** wasn't allowed to play the game.

_____ **c)** didn't have a special talent for the game.

4. When a friend tells you that she needs to unwind, she means she needs to:

_____ **a)** get some air.

_____ **b)** lose weight.

_____ **c)** do something relaxing.

5. When Karim says, "I'm dead on my feet," she means:

_____ **a)** She's dying.

_____ **b)** She's very tired.

_____ **c)** Her feet hurt.

6. When I say that something doesn't make sense, I mean that:

204

_____ **a)** It's not easy.

_____ **b)** It's not difficult.

_____ **c)** It's not logical.

7. When we speak about state-of-the-art equipment we mean that:

_____ **a)** It's the most highly developed.

_____ **b)** It's concerned with the arts.

_____ **c)** It's owned by the state.

8. When the doctor tells you that you have to cut down on red meat, she means you have to:

_____ **a)** stop eating meat.

_____ **b)** eat chopped meat.

_____ **c)** eat less meat.

9. If I say that when I go jogging I wear out very quickly I mean:

_____ **a)** I get tired.

_____ **b)** I warm up.

_____ **c)** I start out fast.

10. If I tell you that I've put on weight, I mean that:

_____ **a)** I've gained weight.

_____ **b)** I've lost weight.

_____ **c)** I've maintained my weight.

LESSON 10

Part I

We're going to read some dialogues using some of the vocabulary items from this lesson. On your answer sheet there are three possible answers for each question. Put a check beside the letter of the answer you think is the best.

1. **A:** Now that you're getting over your cold, would you like to go out to dinner tomorrow night?

    B: Thanks, Bill, but I don't feel up to it yet.

In this dialogue, "I don't feel up to it" means:

    ____ **a)** I'd rather eat at home.

    ____ **b)** I'm not well enough yet.

    ____ **c)** I don't have any appetite yet.

2. **A:** Hi, Tom. How's your father doing?

    B: He's a little under the weather these days.

In this dialogue, "He's a little under the weather" means:

    ____ **a)** He's not feeling as well as he usually does.

    ____ **b)** He's fine but he doesn't like the weather.

    ____ **c)** The weather makes him feel sick.

3. **A:** Is your grandfather still in the hospital?

    B: Yes, he is. He's recuperating slowly.

In this dialogue, "recuperating" means:

    ____ **a)** He's getting worse.

    ____ **b)** He's getting tired.

    ____ **c)** He's getting well.

4. **A:** What's the matter? Are you ill?

    B: I'm dizzy. I'd better sit down.

In this dialogue, the word "dizzy" means:

    ____ **a)** I feel silly.

    ____ **b)** I'm unsteady on my feet.

    ____ **c)** I'm tired of standing up.

5. **A:** Did you go to the doctor this afternoon?

    B: Yes, and he checked me over thoroughly.

In this dialogue, the expression "checked me over" means:

_____ **a)** He gave me a complete examination.

_____ **b)** He passed me along to another doctor.

_____ **c)** He asked me to pay him by check.

Part II

Now you're going to hear some sentences which contain some two-word verbs you have studied in this lesson. I'll read each sentence twice. Just listen the first time. When I read the sentence the second time, put a check on the line to the left of the word or statement which best expresses the meaning of the verb used in the sentence.

1. When I say that I ran out of the pills I take for my allergy, I mean:

_____ **a)** I went to buy some.

_____ **b)** I used all of them.

_____ **c)** I threw them away.

2. I think I'm coming down with a cold means:

_____ **a)** I'm getting a cold.

_____ **b)** I'm getting over a cold.

_____ **c)** I'm taking care of a cold.

3. When I tell you that Eli had a dangerous operation but that he pulled through, I mean he:

_____ **a)** survived it.

_____ **b)** died from it.

_____ **c)** avoided it.

4. A flu epidemic often breaks out during the winter months means that the epidemic:

_____ **a)** ends.

_____ **b)** continues.

_____ **c)** occurs.

5. When I say that my arthritis is acting up today, I mean that my arthritis:

_____ **a)** is getting better.

_____ **b)** is painful.

_____ **c)** is not bothering me.

LESSON 11

The sentences you are going to hear contain some of the expressions you have studied in this lesson. I'll read each sentence twice. Just listen the first time. When I read the sentence the second time, put a check on the line to the left of the sentence or phrase you think gives the best meaning of the expression used in the sentence.

1. "Mary is putting on her clothes right now" means Mary is:

_____ **a)** getting undressed.

_____ **b)** trying on new clothes.

_____ **c)** getting dressed.

2. If I say, "Those are pretty shoes you have on," I mean:

_____ **a)** You are wearing them.

_____ **b)** You own them.

_____ **c)** You need them.

3. When a customer says, "That blouse is pretty but it's not what I had in mind; thank you anyway," she means that:

_____ **a)** She's not going to buy the blouse.

_____ **b)** It's not what she was looking for, but she'll buy it anyway.

_____ **c)** She likes the blouse and she may buy it later.

4. When I say, "That color is very becoming to you," I am speaking to:

_____ **a)** a man.

_____ **b)** a woman.

_____ **c)** either a man or a woman.

5. The sentence, "When I have time to kill, I like to go window shopping," means that I go window shopping when:

_____ **a)** I have something to do but I'll do it later.

_____ **b)** There is nothing special that I have to do.

_____ **c)** I don't feel like buying anything.

6. When I say, "You look very well in that color," I am speaking:

_____ **a)** only to a man.

_____ **b)** only to a woman.

_____ **c)** to either a man or a woman.

7. John is always so well-groomed means that John is always:

_____ **a)** expensively dressed.

_____ **b)** carefully dressed.

_____ **c)** very fashionably dressed.

8. When I say that my kid brother doesn't like to get dressed up I mean that he doesn't like to:

_____ **a)** wear any clothes.

_____ **b)** wear elegant clothes.

_____ **c)** wear his old clothes.

9. When I want to exchange an item and the salesperson says, "Do you have the sales slip?" she is asking whether I:

_____ **a)** have proof that I bought the item.

_____ **b)** want a refund.

_____ **c)** know the price of the item.

10. When an article is for sale, it is:

_____ **a)** being sold at a lower price than usual.

_____ **b)** there for people to buy.

_____ **c)** only there for people to look at.

LESSON 12

The dialogues you will hear contain some of the expressions or words you have learned in this lesson. We'll read each dialogue twice. Just listen the first time. When you hear the dialogue the second time, put a check mark next to the word or expression that best explains the one used in the dialogue.

1. A: We really need a new car. Ours is practically falling apart.

   B: I know we do, but we can't afford one right now.

In this dialogue, the expression **can't afford** means we:

    ____ **a)** don't have to pay cash for it.

    ____ **b)** don't want to borrow money for it.

    ____ **c)** don't have the money for it.

2. A: Why are you so depressed?

   B: Because I just can't seem to make ends meet anymore.

In this dialogue, the expression **make ends meet** means:

    ____ **a)** fasten my belt.

    ____ **b)** bring the two pieces together.

    ____ **c)** manage to live on my income.

3. A: Guess what? I'll be getting a raise next month.

   B: Hey, that's great news. Congratulations! You deserve it.

In this dialogue, "I'll be getting a raise" means I'll:

    ____ **a)** be paid more money for doing my job.

    ____ **b)** be starting a new job.

    ____ **c)** be awarded a prize for weight lifting.

4. A: I see Jack finally paid you the money he's owed for months.

   B: Yes, but unfortunately, his check bounced.

In this dialogue, "his check bounced" means that the check:

_____ **a)** was made of rubber.

_____ **b)** was returned for insufficient funds.

_____ **c)** was stolen.

5. **A:** I hear you have a new job. How much will you make?

   B: I'm not exactly sure yet. I'll know by the end of this week.

In this dialogue, the word **make** means how much you will:

_____ **a)** be paid.

_____ **b)** produce.

_____ **c)** be able to save.

6. **A:** Did you get all your business done at the bank?

   B: Oh, yes. A very nice young man waited on me.

In this dialogue, the expression **waited on** means:

_____ **a)** took care of my business.

_____ **b)** was expecting me.

_____ **c)** asked me for a date.

7. **A:** We don't have enough money in the checking account to pay this bill.

   B: Don't worry. I'll make a deposit this afternoon.

In this dialogue, the expression **make a deposit** means:

_____ **a)** borrow some money.

_____ **b)** put some money in the bank.

_____ **c)** earn some money.

8. **A:** Will Bill get a bonus at the end of the year?

   B: I hope so. He needs it to pay some of his debts.

In this dialogue, the word **bonus** means:

_____ **a)** some extra money.

_____ **b)** some money owed to him.

_____ **c)** an extra job.

9. **A:** All your children are college graduates, aren't they?

    B: Yes, I'm very proud of them. They're all doing very well.

In this dialogue, the expression **doing very well** means:

    ____ **a)** healthy.

    ____ **b)** successful.

    ____ **c)** happy.

10. **A:** Congratulations on your promotion! Will you be getting a higher salary?

    B: Yes, but, unfortunately, it won't make much difference in my take-home pay.

In this dialogue, the expression **take-home pay** means:

    ____ **a)** salary minus taxes and other deductions.

    ____ **b)** salary plus some extra money.

    ____ **c)** money I can earn at home.

LESSON 13

The sentences you are going to hear contain some of the two-word verbs and expressions you have studied in this lesson. I'll read each sentence twice. Just listen the first time. When I read the sentence the second time, put a check on the line to the left of the statement or phrase which best expresses the meaning of the verb or expression used in the sentence.

1. If I tell you to get off the bus at 42nd Street, I want you to:

    ____ **a)** enter the bus.

    ____ **b)** leave the bus.

    ____ **c)** stay on the bus.

2. If I say that the train was so crowded that I couldn't get on, I mean I couldn't:

    ____ **a)** leave the train.

    ____ **b)** stay on the train.

    ____ **c)** enter the train.

3. If I say we have to pick up our luggage after we leave the plane, I mean we have to:

____ **a)** collect our luggage.

____ **b)** buy our luggage.

____ **c)** drop off our luggage.

4. If I say that the plane is going to take off any minute now, I mean that the plane:

____ **a)** is going to leave the ground.

____ **b)** is going to fall to the ground.

____ **c)** is going to return to the terminal.

5. When I say that if you don't confirm your reservation you may run into a problem, I mean that you may:

____ **a)** solve a problem.

____ **b)** have a problem.

____ **c)** eliminate a problem.

6. If a woman is giving you directions on how to get to a place and she says, "You can't miss it," she means you can't:

____ **a)** fail to make it.

____ **b)** fail to hit it.

____ **c)** fail to see it.

7. If your friend asks you to go to a concert and says, "Let's go Dutch," this person means that:

____ **a)** You'll each pay for your own ticket.

____ **b)** You'll pay for your friend's ticket.

____ **c)** You'll use a credit card.

8. If your friend tells you that his father had a reservation for a flight but he was bumped off it, he means his father:

____ **a)** was hit with something.

____ **b)** was killed.

____ **c)** was taken off the flight.

9. If you feel butterflies in your stomach you:

_____ **a)** have a stomachache.

_____ **b)** are nervous.

_____ **c)** are happy.

10. When your travel agent tells you that you must check into the hotel before midnight, that person means you have to:

_____ **a)** pay the hotel.

_____ **b)** call the hotel.

_____ **c)** register at the hotel.

REVIEW LESSON II

We're going to read some dialogues using vocabulary items from Lessons 8 through 13. On your answer sheet you'll find three possible answers for each question. Put a check next to the answer you think is correct. Each dialogue will be read twice.

1. **A:** What happened to Lorraine?
   B: She passed out while she was playing tennis.

In this dialogue, the word **passed out** means:

_____ **a)** lost consciousness.

_____ **b)** left the tennis court.

_____ **c)** hit the ball too hard.

2. **A:** Those are pretty shoes. I'll bet they were expensive.
   B: They were. I'll have to be careful with them so they won't wear out too soon.

In this dialogue, the expression **wear out** means:

_____ **a)** become unusable.

_____ **b)** be wearable outside.

_____ **c)** go out of style.

3. **A:** There's practically nothing in the refrigerator.
   B: We'll just have to eat leftovers, I guess.

In this dialogue, the word **leftovers** means:

    ____ **a)** food someone else threw out.

    ____ **b)** food that was overcooked.

    ____ **c)** food remaining from a previous meal.

4. **A:** What's the matter? Did you lose something?

    B: I just made a deposit and now I can't find my passbook.

In this dialogue, the word **passbook** means:

    ____ **a)** a book of coupons for free admission to a sports event.

    ____ **b)** a record of a savings account.

    ____ **c)** a document required for international travel.

5. **A:** Billy has been getting very good grades in elementary school.

    B: Great! Let's hope he keeps it up.

In this dialogue, the expression **keeps it up** means:

    ____ **a)** continues as he is doing.

    ____ **b)** tries to get even better grades.

    ____ **c)** saves all his report cards.

6. **A:** What did you do last Saturday afternoon? I tried to call you but you weren't home.

    B: I went window shopping with my father at the shopping center.

In this dialogue, **window shopping** means:

    ____ **a)** buying new windows for our house.

    ____ **b)** looking at merchandise on display in store windows.

    ____ **c)** buying something displayed in a store window.

7. **A:** I'll bet Patty got all dressed up for her birthday party last week.

    B: She looked very pretty. She had on a beautiful green silk dress.

In this dialogue, the word **had on** means:

    ____ **a)** bought.

    ____ **b)** borrowed.

    ____ **c)** wore.

8. **A:** How is your sister? I haven't seen her in a long time.

   B: Well, right now, she's just getting over a serious operation.

In this dialogue, the word **getting over** means:

_____ **a)** recovering from.

_____ **b)** preparing for.

_____ **c)** going through.

9. **A:** Do you remember the recipe for that wonderful beef stew your father used to make?

   B: No, I don't, but I can look it up. I'll call you back.

In this dialogue, the word **recipe** refers to:

_____ **a)** a list of ingredients for the stew.

_____ **b)** the cost of making the stew.

_____ **c)** the name of the stew.

10. **A:** Did it take your parents long to collect their baggage?

   B: No, they always travel light when they come for a weekend.

In this dialogue, the expression **travel light** means:

_____ **a)** carry only a little baggage.

_____ **b)** travel during the daylight hours.

_____ **c)** carry light-colored suitcases.

11. **A:** I hear you and your wife are flying to Europe.

   B: Yes, we're taking an excursion next month.

In this dialogue, the word **excursion** means:

_____ **a)** student group.

_____ **b)** cruise.

_____ **c)** pleasure trip.

12. **A:** Did your doctor put you on a special diet?

   B: No, he just told me to eat only lean meat and lots of vegetables.

In this dialogue the expression **lean meat** refers to meat that is:

_____ **a)** fresh.

_____ **b)** not fatty.

_____ **c)** well-cooked.

13. **A:** When you were a child, who took care of you when you were sick?

B: My grandmother. She always found a remedy for whatever we had.

In this dialogue, the word **remedy** means:

_____ **a)** cure.

_____ **b)** reason.

_____ **c)** doctor.

14. **A:** How much did Jim pay for all that cement?

B: I don't know. I didn't see the invoice.

In this dialogue, the word **invoice** means:

_____ **a)** receipt.

_____ **b)** check.

_____ **c)** bill.

15. **A:** That dress is very becoming to Mary, isn't it?

B: Yes. It makes her look really slender.

In this dialogue, the word **slender** means:

_____ **a)** slim.

_____ **b)** young.

_____ **c)** tall.

Appendix

I. CARDINAL NUMBERS

A. Definition

The cardinal numbers are the numbers which we use when we want to enumerate, to count units, or to indicate quantity. Odd numbers are 1, 3, 5, 7, etc. Even numbers are 2, 4, 6, 8, etc.

B. Rules for Cardinal Numbers

Each language has its own way of expressing combinations of cardinal numbers. Let us look at the rules which govern numbers in English.

1. EXPRESSING NUMBERS

a. Hundreds

179	one hundred seventy-nine or a hundred and seventy-nine
306	three hundred six or three hundred and six
895	eight hundred ninety-five or eight hundred and ninety-five

b. Thousands, ten thousands, hundred thousands

2,083	two thousand, eighty-three
31,127	thirty-one thousand, one hundred twenty-seven
725,651	seven hundred twenty-five thousand, six hundred fifty-one

> **NOTE:** When the thousand numeral is followed by any digit between one and nine and two zeros, the numbers are sometimes expressed in the hundreds.

2,100	two thousand, one hundred or twenty-one hundred
1,800	one thousand, eight hundred or eighteen hundred
9,700	nine thousand, seven hundred or ninety-seven hundred

c. Millions and billions

1,410,326	one million, four hundred ten thousand, three hundred twenty-six
22,200,000	twenty-two million, two hundred thousand
890,375,203	eight hundred ninety million, three hundred seventy-five thousand, two hundred three
12,639,000,000	twelve billion, six hundred, thirty-nine million

2. TELEPHONE NUMBERS

These are usually expressed individually in digits.

The area code is also given in digits.

725-1036	seven two five, one o three six (zero may be expressed in place of the letter o)
781-9674	seven eight one, nine six seven four
761-0200	seven six one, o two hundred
763-5000	seven six three, five thousand
(809) 763-4258	eight o nine, seven six three, four two five eight

3. STUDENT IDENTIFICATION NUMBER (OR ANY IDENTIFICATION NUMBER)

These are also expressed in digits.

801-79-5332	eight o one, seven nine, five three three two
586-20-4587	five eight six, two o, four five eight seven
748-81-5063	seven four eight, eight one, five o six three

4. COURSE NUMBERS

When the number contains three digits, it is divided into two units. If a zero appears as a middle digit, it is read like the letter o, and the number is read in three units.

English 109	one o nine
Chemistry 324	three twenty-four
Mathematics 2331	twenty-three thirty-one

5. FLIGHT NUMBERS

These combinations are expressed like course numbers.

Flight 333	three thirty-three
Flight 401	four o one
Flight 1031	ten thirty-one

6. ADDRESSES

An address number may contain up to five digits which may be expressed in units of two. When there is a zero you may express it as the letter o unless it makes up a unit of ten, hundred, or thousand.

7 Lily Street (St.)	seven
47 Ford Avenue (Ave.)	forty-seven
460 Sunset Boulevard (Blvd.)	four-sixty
4635 Ocean Drive (Dr.)	forty-six thirty-five
81359 Greenville Road (Rd.)	eighty-one three fifty-nine

105 Shady Lane	one o five
2300 Kennedy Avenue (Ave.)	twenty-three hundred
6000 Fourth Avenue (Ave.)	six thousand

> **NOTE:** Notice the correct order of items in the addresses above. Below you will find some examples of the correct order of addresses in which additional information is necessary. Notice that ZIP Codes are expressed in digits.

13 Elm Street	thirteen
Pacific Manor, Apt. 307	three o seven
Santurce, Puerto Rico 00907	o, o, nine o seven
46 West 147 Street	one hundred forty-seventh
New York, New York 11036	
75-57 168 Street*	one hundred sixty-eight
Forest Hills, New York 11374	
P. O. Box 22085	post office box two two o eight five**
Belleville, Illinois 66037	

The digit box numbers are expressed:

Box 315	three fifteen
407	four o seven

7. YEARS

Years with four digits are expressed in two units.

| 1925 | nineteen twenty-five |
| 1889 | eighteen eighty-nine |

When the year with four digits has an even hundred or thousand, it may be expressed as follows.

| 1800 | eighteen hundred |
| 2000 | two thousand |

When a zero precedes the last of four digits, the zero may be expressed as o.

| 1506 | fifteen o six *or* fifteen hundred six |

---

* Use ordinal numbers for avenue, road, and street numbers when they are part of an address. However, when speaking of a highway with a number, you would refer to it as Route 247 (two forty-seven) or simply 247. In other words, use ordinal numbers before a noun; use cardinal numbers after a noun.

** Box numbers are expressed in digits when they have more than three digits.

Years with fewer than four digits are expressed in tens or hundreds or in two units.

25	twenty-five
500	five hundred
711	seven hundred eleven *or* seven eleven

To identify the era, simply add B.C. after the year for the era before Christ, and A.D. for the era after Christ.

2000 B.C.   52 B.C.   52 A.D.   2000 A.D.

8. SIGNS, SYMBOLS, AND ABBREVIATIONS

+	plus		no.	number
−	minus		min.	minute
x	times, by*		hr.	hour
÷	divided by		wk.	week
=	equals, is equal to		mo.	month
#	number		yr.	year
%	percent			
			in.	inches
$	dollar		ft.	foot, feet
¢	cent		yd.	yard
°	degree		doz.	dozen
'	feet			
"	inches		oz.	ounce
/	per, a, an		lb.	pound
			pt.	pint
C	Celsius (also centigrade)		gal.	gallon
F	Fahrenheit		gr.	gram
S	South**		kg.	kilogram
N	North		lt.	liter
W	West			
E	East		m.	meter
SW	Southwest		mm.	millimeter
SE	Southeast		cm.	centimeter
NW	Northwest		dm.	decimeter
NE	Northeast		km.	kilometer
			ml.	mile

---

* "3 x 3 = 9" is read: "Three times three equals nine."
"The room measures 10' x 12'" is read: "The room measures ten feet by twelve feet," or simply "ten by twelve."

** When the words **North**, **South**, **Northeast**, **Southwest**, etc., are used as the name of a geographic area they are capitalized. When used to indicate a direction, they are *not* capitalized.

Examples: The West was the last part of the United States to be developed.
Nebraska is west of the Mississippi River.

C. Exercises Using Cardinal Numbers

READING NUMBERS

a. 1. Count by twos to thirty
   2. Count by even numbers to 20
   3. Count by odd numbers to 19
   4. Count by fives to 50

b. 1. 1,250
   2. 4,387
   3. 55,394
   4. 39,014
   5. 805,312
   6. 525,307
   7. 3,500
   8. 1,002
   9. 9,900
   10. 743,123
   11. 5,050
   12. 105,006
   13. 280,704
   14. 75,467
   15. 280,017
   16. 2,375,416
   17. 4,900,303
   18. 65,117,787
   19. 342,321,218
   20. 5,300,000,000

c. **Telephone numbers**
   1. 752-0075
   2. 833-9164
   3. 644-5000
   4. 764-5006
   5. 532-7849
   6. 803-724-6879

d. **Student identification numbers**
   1. 467-83-5487
   2. 249-87-7497
   3. 300-78-4000
   4. 801-54-9462
   5. 543-71-3496

e. **Course numbers**
   1. History 320
   2. English 2332
   3. Spanish 3412
   4. Biology 201
   5. Anthropology 125
   6. Fine Arts 4572

    f.   **Flight numbers**

       1. Flight 243

       2. Flight 47

       3. Flight 302

       4. Flight 4165

    g.   **Dates**

       1. 35 B.C.

       2. 520 A.D.

       3. 1600

       4. 1980

       5. 1000

       6. 1066

       7. 300 B.C.

       8. 350 A.D.

       9. 1905

     10. 1898

     11. 1100

     12. 6000 B.C.

     13. She was born in 1802.

     14. Columbus discovered America in 1492.

D. Reading Symbols and Abbreviations

Read the following phrases and expressions. Some expressions can be read two ways.

  1. Fifteen plus fifteen equals thirty. ($15 + 15 = 30$)

  2. Twenty minus three is equal to seventeen. ($20 - 3 = 17$)

  3. Nine times five equals forty-five. ($9 \times 5 = 45$)

  4. Thirty-six divided by four is equal to nine. ($36 \div 4 = 9$)

  5. Thirty-three, dash, seventy-two, dash, seventy-eight. (33–72–78)

  6. Fifty-one percent. (51%)

  7. Twenty-seven dollars and fifty cents. ($27.50)

  8. Six feet, two inches. (6' 2")

  9. Five ounces. (5 oz.)

 10. Seventeen miles. (17 ml.)

 11. Sixteen pounds. (16 lbs.)

 12. Seven quarts. (7 qts.)

 13. Three liters. (3 lts.)

 14. Sixty-five pounds. (65 lbs.)

 15. Eighteen gallons. (18 gal.)

Now read the following items.

1.	.75	**9.**	17.6 lts.
2.	5 ft. 3 in.	**10.**	1 doz.
3.	53.2°C	**11.**	14 yrs.
4.	7.5%	**12.**	6 mos.
5.	25 kg.	**13.**	13 wks.
6.	2 km.	**14.**	24 hrs.
7.	98.6°F	**15.**	2 min.
8.	19 yds.	**16.**	.065

E. Mini-Dialogues

Listen carefully as your instructor reads each of these dialogues. Then read them aloud according to your instructor's directions.

1. **A:** We need some information from you. How old are you?

B: I'm 19 years old.

A: How tall are you?

B: I'm 5 feet, 6 inches tall. (*Also:* I'm 5'6" *or* I'm five foot six.)

A: And how much do you weigh?

B: I weigh 117 pounds.

A: Thank you. That's all for now. Please take a seat until your name is called.

2. **A:** When were you born?

B: I was born in 1957.

A: In what city?

B: I was born in Paris.

3. **A:** How many days does February have?

B: 29 days.

A: But that's in a leap year.

B: Oh! That's right. It usually has only 28 days.

4. **A:** Hi, Louise, I heard you just bought an apartment. Is it big?

B: It has three bedrooms, two baths, a living room, dining area, and kitchen.

A: Was it expensive?

B: *Very* expensive. It cost $95,000.

5. **A:** Operator, could you please give me the number of International Cable?

    B: One moment, please.

    A: Thank you.

    B: The number is 784-5321.

    A: (Slowly, as if writing it down.) 784-5321. Thank you, operator.

6. **A:** What's the phone number of Lifetime Insurance Company?

    B: Their main office?

    A: Yes, the one on Central Avenue.

    B: The number is 835-6825 or 835-6826.

    A: 835-6825 or 835-6826. (Slowly.) Thank you, operator.

7. **A:** Hello. Is Sue in?

    B: What number are you calling?

    A: 724-6833.

    B: Sorry, you have the wrong number.

8. **A:** José, you're not on the list of students registered in Section 13.

    B: But I did register. Here's my program card.

    A: Give me your student number and I'll add your name to the list.

    B: It's 801-91-7235.

    A: 801-91-7235. Thank you, José.

9. **A:** What's your favorite course this semester?

    B: Chemistry 1246. What's yours?

    A: I prefer Biology 2011. It's much more interesting.

    B: I like chemistry better! It's my major subject.

10. **A:** Could you lend me 50 cents until tomorrow? I forgot my wallet.

    B: Of course. Are you sure 50 cents is enough?

    A: Yes, I missed my ride home. I just need bus fare.

    B: Oh, come on. I'll be glad to give you a ride.

11. **A:** May I help you?

    B: Yes, thank you. How much are these ties?

    A: This one is $10.50 and that one is $15.99.

    B: I'll take that one. Would you please gift-wrap it?

    A: Certainly.

12. **A:** Good morning. Is there a sale on jackets?

B: Yes. There's a 15% discount on all merchandise.

A: Oh! Everything is half-price.

B: No, I said fifteen percent, not fifty percent.

F. Asking Questions

Ask the student who sits next to you the following questions according to your instructor's instructions. Answer in complete sentences.

1. How old are you?
2. In what year were you born? (*Alternate:* When were you born?) (Remember to use the proposition **in** before the year.)
3. When are you planning to graduate?
4. When did you graduate from high school?
5. What is your student number?
6. What are the two (easiest, most interesting, most difficult) courses you are taking this semester?
7. What is your complete address? (Include your ZIP Code.)
8. What is your telephone number? (If you don't have a telephone, give a friend's number or make up a number.)
9. Name a year that was very important in your life and tell why.
10. What was the temperature yesterday?
11. What is the speed limit on most of the highways?
12. What is the approximate size of this classroom?
13. How many students are there is this class?
14. How much gasoline does your car's gas tank hold?

II. THE ORDINAL NUMBERS

A. Definition

The ordinal numbers indicate the order or position in a series, as in the following example: There is an **X** in the third box. (Whenever a number is used as an adjective or when it answers the question which one? about the following word, that number must be an ordinal number.)

Example: Which box has the **X**?   *Answer:* The **third** box.

☐   ☐   ☒

B. Rules for Ordinal Numbers

1. FRACTIONS

Use ordinal numbers to express fractions.

1/3	one third	1/4	one fourth
2/3	two thirds	3/4	three fourths
1/5	one fifth	3/8	three eighths
4/5	four fifths	9/16	nine sixteenths

> **NOTE:** 1/2 is expressed as **one half** (the **l** is silent.)

2. DATES

Notice how the following dates are expressed. The number of the day of the month is always expressed as an ordinal number and the year as a cardinal number. When used in a phrase or sentence, the date is preceded by the preposition **on**.

August 5, 1932	August fifth, nineteen thirty-two
February 2, 1785	February second, seventeen eighty-five
January 3, 1803	January third, eighteen hundred three, *or* eighteen o three, *or* eighteen three

Below you will find the months of the year and their abbreviations.

January	Jan.	July	Jul.
February	Feb.	August	Aug.
March	Mar.	September	Sept.
April	Apr.	October	Oct.
May	May	November	Nov.
June	Je.	December	Dec.*

The seasons are: spring, summer, autumn (fall), and winter.

3. OTHER USES OF ORDINAL NUMBERS

a. Streets, roads, avenues

I live on Third Avenue.

We're moving to 102nd Street. (one hundred second)

The club is on 218th Street. (two hundred eighteenth)

---

* The months and their abbreviations are written with capital letters. The seasons are written with small letters.

b.   Division in games

They played up to the tenth inning.

This is just the first quarter.

c.   Anniversaries, birthdays

Next year my parents celebrate their fiftieth wedding anniversary.

She had a party for her fifteenth birthday.

d.   Floors, rows, aisles, seats (Note the prepositions used.)

I live **on** the ninth floor.

We were sitting **in** the fifth row **in** the theater.

I prefer to have a seat **on** the aisle so I can leave quickly after the show.

I got tickets **for** the first and second seats **in** row AA.

e.   School grade, college year

My brother is **in** the third grade.

This is my first year **of** college.

NOTE: The following terminology is also used in English to refer to the years in high school and college:

1st—freshman year	3rd—junior year
2nd—sophomore year	4th—senior year

---

f.   Line of succession

John F. Kennedy was the 35th* president of the United States.

Mr. Frank was the third principal of this school.

g.   Vertical and horizontal order

Did you recognize me in the photograph?

I'm the tenth from the right.

Your name appears in the second line from the bottom.

C.   Exercises Using Ordinal Numbers

1.   Change the following cardinal numbers to ordinal numbers.

1	2	93	89	103	33
13	32	101	405	55	142

---

* In formal written English, this word is **thirty-fifth**.

2. Read the following items.

| 7/12 | 5/16 | 3/5 | 3/4 | 2-3/8 |
| 5/8 | 2/3 | 1/2 | 11/3 | 13-7/16 |

3. Read the following dates.

January 12, 1974	November 3, 1980
October 9, 1941	December 23, 2000
July 31, 1938	May 3, 1969
March 5, 1900	August 21, 1514
September 1, 1605	June 14, 1749
April 25, 1843	February 22, 1898

4. Read the following sentences. (Note the prepositions used.)

1. The shoe store is located **on** 65th Infantry Road.
2. We left the game **in** the 7th* inning.
3. I just celebrated my twenty-first birthday.
4. In this photograph, Mariel is the first one **on** the right.
5. James is sitting **in** the sixth seat **in** the first row.
6. Neil Armstrong was the first man **on** the moon.
7. Jackie is a student **in** the fifth grade.

D. Additional Exercises Using Ordinal Numbers

Ask the student next to you the following questions according to your instructor's directions.

1. What is your birth date?
2. When is your birthday?
3. What's the date today?
4. What was the date yesterday?
5. What day is today?
6. In which row do you sit in the Speech Laboratory?
7. Which grade of elementary or high school did you enjoy most?
8. What year of school are you in?
9. Which birthday do you celebrate this year?
10. Which floor do you have to go to after your English class?

---

* In formal written English, this word is written **seventh**.

III. REVIEW OF NUMBERS

A. Answer these questions in complete sentences.

1. When is your mother's birthday?
2. What is your father's birth date?
3. On what date is Christmas Day?
4. When is Labor Day celebrated?
5. On what date is Halloween celebrated?
6. On which Thursday in November is Thanksgiving celebrated?
7. Which Sunday in May is Mother's Day?
8. What is the age of the oldest member of your family? The youngest?
9. What will the date be one week from today?
10. What was the date the day before yesterday?
11. What will the date be the day after tomorrow?
12. What was the decade before the present one called?
13. What was the date a week ago yesterday?
14. What will the next century be?
15. In which century was America discovered?

B. A review of various combinations of numbers.

1. Read these telephone numbers:

   753-6130
   765-5400
   589-5069
   763-6003

2. Ask the person on your right for his or her complete address, including the ZIP Code number.

3. Ask the person next to you for his or her student number.

4. Give the ordinal number for these cardinal numbers:

   thirty-three   sixty-five   twenty-one   fifty-two   twenty

5. Read these dates:

   June 1, 1903   May 3, 1753   February 25, 1930

6. Read these numbers:

17,007,715

231,016,005

5,603,760

516,700,005

7. Read these fractions:

3/4

7/8

15/16

7/32

4/5

2/3

1/2

8. Read these temperatures:

215°C

198.6°F

30.7°C

9. Read the following:

$2 \times 15 =$ _____

$144 \div 12 =$ _____

$15 + 16 =$ _____

$230 - 17 =$ _____

10. The room measures 10' 6" x 15' 10".

11. Count by odd numbers to 20.

12. Count by even numbers to twenty.

13. 2300 W. 16th Street

1501 42nd Street

345 N. 53rd Ave.

201 Washington Rd.

14. I'm taking Biology 315 and Chemistry 201 next semester.

15. The price of that dress has been reduced from $49.95 to $32.50.

PHOTO CREDITS

p. 1 — *Top right:* Ken Karp
Top left: Laima Druskis
Bottom: Ken Karp

p. 16 — *All:* Laima Druskis

p. 29 — *Bottom left:* Laima Druskis
Bottom right: Marc Anderson

p. 42 — *Top right and left:* Laima Druskis
Bottom: Ken Karp

p. 56 — *Top right:* Eugene Gordon
Top left: Shirley Zeiberg
Middle: National Institute on Aging
Bottom: United Nations photo 148562 by Bruno J. Zehnder

p. 67 — *Top right, top left, and bottom right:* Laima Druskis
Bottom left: Ken Karp

p. 79 — Jay Seeley

p. 86 — *Top left:* Eugene Gordon
Top right: Teri Leigh Stratford
Bottom: Laima Druskis

p. 101 — *Top right:* Courtesy of Squibb Corporation
Bottom: Laima Druskis

p. 114 — *Bottom:* Eugene Gordon

p. 129 — *All:* Courtesy of Brooks Brothers Clothing

p. 148 — *Top left:* Marc Anderson
Top right: Irene Springer
Bottom: Laima Druskis

p. 162 — *Top:* Courtesy of Greyhound–Trailways Bus Lines
Bottom left: Marc Anderson
Bottom right: Laima Druskis

p. 177 — Ken Karp